A **WESTERN HORSEMAN** BOOK

The Language of Horsemanship

How to Speak "Horse"

Dick Pieper

with Cheryl Magoteaux Cody

Edited by Fran Devereux Smith

The Language of Horsemanship

Published by
WESTERN HORSEMAN magazine
2112 Montgomery St.
Fort Worth, TX 76107
817-737-6397

www.westernhorseman.com

Design, Typography, and Production
Globe Pequot Press
Guilford, Connecticut
and
Candice Noyce
Pro Management Inc.
Byars, Oklahoma

Front Cover Photo by Ross Hecox
Back Cover Photo by Darrell Dodds

Printing
Versa Press, Inc.
East Peoria, Illinois

Manufactured in the United States of America

First Printing: October 2013

ISBN 978-0-7627-9289-4

Dedication and Acknowledgments

This book is dedicated to my lovely wife, Brenda. She truly has been my inspiration and the support behind whatever successes I may have had.

In the 26 years of our marriage, she has taken on the roles of ranch manager, breeding manager, bookkeeper, cook, gardener, housekeeper, financial consultant, tour guide, advertising manager, manager of horse sales, both public and private, and corporate planner. Besides those things and a few I may have overlooked, she does a great job of preparing and starting young horses on cattle. She has probably the best eye for conformation, overall balance and breeding that I have ever seen and is the consummate horsewoman in every respect.

Beyond all of the above, she is my life partner and my very, very best friend.

Dick Pieper

Dick Pieper

Contents

Foreword

For many years, Dick Pieper has been an information source for me. As a young man growing up in California, I read several articles he'd written about the various training strategies of the day. I was trying to absorb all the horse education I could. As I centered my ambitions on cutting horses, I still sought knowledge from Dick and others featured in the performance-horse-discipline magazines. I always was looking for ways to improve myself and add a different slant to training my horses, to help improve them.

I met Dick and Brenda Pieper formally at the Augusta Cutting Horse Futurity. They were there to show their great young stallion Playgun. Dick won the non-pro futurity with the horse, then watched Jody Galyean win the open futurity division with Playgun, catapulting the gray stallion into the limelight of the cutting-horse world. Tap O Lena was 6 years old that year and considered one of the great cutting mares of her day, and the Piepers approached me about breeding her to Playgun when the time came. That was the start of our friendship.

Along with Dick's fine knowledge of general horse-behavior management, he and Brenda also are known for their knowledge of performance-horse conformation and how best to choose horses for conformation that functions well.

This was an area of great interest to me. I knew that I must grasp a better knowledge of conformation if I was to continue improving myself in the horse business. Due to my new friendship with the Piepers and their reputations for understanding conformation, I began to spend many hours discussing equine conformation and horse behavior with them. Our friendship grew from there, and we spent many days looking over prospects either for sale or at my training place. If I asked the questions, usually Dick and Brenda would have the answers. Later I would have the good fortune to assist Dick and Brenda with some of their futurity prospects.

I suggest that anyone who wishes to do anything with a horse should read this book! I have been working with horses since 1978 and I learned several things I did not know until I had read the book myself. I'm making this book mandatory reading for my employees at Rapp Ranch. This book puts a simple outlook to a complicated language spoken to our equine counterparts.

Dick's outlook on various problems created in training horses was put to a real test at my ranch in the summer of 2005. I had a 2-year-old stallion that one of my assistants was having great difficulties with. He had been fighting with the horse for some time and had taught the colt to run to the fence and rub down the side of the fence as a form of release.

Realizing there was a real problem with this colt, I took over his training, and I was in for a real workout! I spent several hours on the ground and on the horse's back trying to remedy the bad habit the horse had developed. One day in particular I was having quite a battle with this colt and he was sure winning!

I was atop this angry, frustrated colt while he propelled himself around the arena fence, my left leg over the top of his neck so I would not have a crushed leg. When I just sat there on him, any time I picked up the reins that colt got angry. I was wondering how to get out of the particular jam I was in.

Just then, in drove this white pickup truck I did not recognize. Out jumped Dick Pieper! "My prayers have been answered!" I thought.

Dick strolled over to the arena, looked in and said, "Howdy, Phil," paused, then said something along these lines, "What kind of problem do you have going on?"

I was so relieved to see Dick! I told him of my problem and asked for some help. I'm glad he didn't ask for money; he could have had part of the ranch at that point! Dick began walking me through a process of adding pressure and releasing it, and in about 30 minutes we had the horse coming our way and staying with the program. After a week of this, the colt never ran to the fence again and later sold for a good price, and went on to become a champion in snaffle-bit competition. As a student of Dick's philosophy, I can tell you with great pride about its benefits!

Read this book, enjoy it, and grasp its information, knowing its contents have been tested and refined through time. Put your own twist to the techniques it teaches and know that every day each of us works with horses is another opportunity to learn something new from our equine counterparts!

Phil Rapp
National Cutting Horse Association
All-Time Leading Rider
First $8-Million Rider
NCHA Riders and Non-Pro Halls of Fame

Western horsemanship has many disciplines. The foundation is the same, no matter if it is reining, cutting, pleasure, roping or trail riding. Dick Piper has been successful as a reiner and as a cutter, and most of all as a horseman.

In this book, Dick is sharing a lifetime of knowledge. This book is necessary reading for anyone who wants to learn about horses from a great horseman.

My hat's off to Dick Pieper for a job well done with horses.

Bob Loomis
National Reining Horse Association
Seven-Time NRHA Futurity Champion
NRHA Hall of Fame

I first met Dick Pieper in September of 1985. I was a young reining-horse trainer eager to take on the world. Dick had come to Pomona, Calif., for one of the first National Reining Horse Association-approved events in the state.

I rode up to him before the first go-round and introduced myself. I can't remember what we talked about, but I remember him being so friendly, inviting, and congenial that I instantly liked him.

At that time Dick and Miss Cee Blair were the absolute best the NRHA open division had. In fact, I would put their 1985 campaign up against any open duo ever. At the end of that weekend competition, Dick had won first and I had won second. That weekend, because I ran neck and neck with Dick and Miss Cee Blair, I learned I could compete with the best—a shot of confidence that some who knew me at the time at the time

probably would say I didn't need—and I had met a man who to this day I admire, respect, and am proud to call my friend.

In *The Language of Horsemanship*, Dick has done the horse industry a great service. He literally takes the reader on a journey of enlightenment on how a true horseman thinks and how horses should be built, not made. Dick is a true horseman and uniquely qualified to write this book. He is a man who has taken countless horses from scratch to major championships, which is the ultimate proof of a program. Some guys start colts well; some guys show well. Dick has done everything in a great way.

Dick also has been a great visionary. When Dick was president of the NRHA, the explosion of reining in Europe started and was nurtured. Dick Pieper was the man who first introduced sons and daughters of Doc O'Lena and Colonel Freckles to the NRHA, forever blurring the lines of reining and cutting pedigrees. It was Dick who plucked Playgun out of a sale in Fort Worth, Texas, when he was a yearling and chose him as a horse to build a program around.

In this wonderful book Dick gives you a foundation program the will make your horse, no matter what the discipline, better than ever. Dick also gives great insight on when and how a horse should be pushed and when you need to back off and be more patient.

We have entered what I call "the age of specialization" within the horse industry. We have horses being bred for specific disciplines and trainers basing their knowledge on a single discipline. One positive of this specialization: It is responsible for producing the number of amazing performances we see in today's horses. However, good overall horsemanship can be lost in this specialized "all-in" mentality.

Through his glorious career as a horseman, few have earned the right to be listened to as much as Dick Pieper. I am thrilled he has spoken in *The Language of Horsemanship*.

Robert Chown
20 Reining and Working Cow Horse
World Titles
American Quarter Horse Association
National Reining Horse Association
National Reined Cow Horse Association
American Paint Horse Association

Preface

We started this book years ago. I had written how-to articles with an A-list of the equine industry's finest but when I worked on an article with Dick Pieper, I was hooked. I'd never met a trainer with his ability to tell exactly what he did, when he did it, why he did it, what to do if I got one response, and what to do with another response.

My recognition that Dick Pieper was a phenomenal communicator with an incredible amount of knowledge and experience made me want to write this book. I knew I'd learn a lot in the process. But I didn't know that working on the book would change my life forever by amending the way I trained or rode a horse. To this day I can hear his voice when I ride. He gave me something precious with horses that I hope comes to every reader of this book.

For the first time ever, when I worked with Dick, the pieces fit together for me. If I used his program from day one and had the basics and used them carefully to create advanced skills, then later correcting a mistake with a horse was simply a matter of considering which of the basics needed reinforcing. Because I methodically followed his program, and listened to the horse's part of the conversation, I always had the tools that fixed any problems.

Finally, my training and riding had a continuity that gave me so much confidence. I didn't have to wonder what was going wrong with a horse or try to watch other people to figure out what to do to fix my problem. I knew that no one knew my horse more than me and no one knew better than I where we'd been or where we were going. If I stayed consistent with my program, I always knew exactly what to do.

I didn't just write about Dick's program, I used it—and the more we worked on the book, the more I became convinced that it should be mandatory reading for anyone who rides horses.

Although Dick and I really wanted to get this book finished, it somehow stayed a work in progress for years. We'd get started, then get sidetracked by our busy lives, and put the book aside for a year or two. Throughout, I never wavered in my opinion of the book, nor of the trainer.

Read this book; absorb its message. Live this method of training a horse and you, like me, will be forever convinced. Your horses will thank you for it.

Cheryl Cody

Cheryl Magoteaux Cody

Introduction

The first challenge for the trainer is to decide what kind of language—which way of communicating—is most effective. The language has to be easily understood by that horse, so we have to base our language on his capabilities.

If you want to communicate with someone from a foreign country, you study him—his customs, habits and society. The more you learn about him, the better you can converse with him.

To be successful in working with horses, we have to understand their culture, too. As the dominant half of the relationship, we use our knowledge of horses and their natures to initiate and control our interactions with them—and to create and teach to them a language they can understand. To do this effectively, we have to be aware of these things.

The horse always has reacted to stress or danger by running quickly away. His speed in flight has been his protection against predators. Since the rider has restricted the horse's ability to flee from danger, the rider must replace the horse's natural fear with confidence and trust.

The horse has developed the ability to react quickly. The same quick reflexes that once helped protect him now let him respond immediately to a stimulus. The rider can count on those reflexes to allow the horse to make lightning-quick responses to the rider's cues.

The horse has a highly developed aptitude for differentiation. That means he can detect even the slightest changes in his environment that might have, in earlier times, meant danger. In modern interaction with humans, this differentiation mechanism enables the horse to clearly recognize and respond quickly to highly sophisticated cues. Tiny movements and changes in position are clearly recognized by the horse. The rider must exactly duplicate his cues and movements because unless he does, the horse sees the movements and cues as not the same.

The horse learns by repetition. Repetition allows a response to become an automatic reaction. So, to train a horse, the rider must cue in exactly the same way each time and he also must repeat that exact cue over and over again.

The horse is secure with consistency and repetition but he is stressed by change or discrepancies. Because of his makeup, he can't evaluate those changes, or deduce the causes, but because of his heightened ability to differentiate, he is supremely aware of them. Even if he is domesticated enough to mind his manners and show no outward response to a change, the inconsistency stresses him because throughout time inconsistency has signaled danger. The rider knows that uniform, repetitive cues and requests and predictable movements and motions can have a calming effect on the horse. Not only does the horse learn through exact repetition, he is reassured by its consistency. It's much more difficult for a horse to learn if he is stressed or confused.

The horse is a herd animal, comfortable with his place in a pecking-order-defined society. A horse is not like a person. He doesn't have to explain to "Mom" why he's not "leadership material." No horse gets an ulcer in the pasture because he's not the boss of all the other horses. Once he understands the pecking order, that's okay with him, regardless of his place in line. He's comfortable with having a boss, having direction and following a familiar routine of obedience.

The rider must be the dominant one in that relationship. If the handler is the boss all the time, the horse is comfortable. If the rider is in charge only part of the time, that inconsistency translates to stress for the horse.

The horse is sensitive to body language. Horses have their own way of communication with one another and body language plays a strong role in equine conversation. Study horses as they interact. For example, when a horse briskly walks straight at another horse, looking at him, that is an aggressive behavior. If you approach a horse in the same manner, he's wary and interprets your actions in the same way. A quick movement from another horse is usually followed by a bite or a kick. The rider must understand that his own movements and posture play a big part in communicating with the horse.

Knowing these things, the rider has the responsibility of controlling the horse's environment in a way that gives him security. The rider must recognize and make intelligent use of all the horse's natural instincts and responses.

The rider must control himself to prevent being influenced by outside factors like anger, frustration, time schedule, emotions, or any other interruptions that the horse cannot understand.

The rider must exactly duplicate his cues and actions each time he works with the horse.

The rider's interaction with the horse can have a calming effect if the rider is consistent and repetitive. The rider also must control the situation so that the horse is not influenced or distracted by outside factors such as pain, sex, anger or hunger.

Most importantly, the rider must respond to the horse's part in the conversation.

If the rider can do all those things, then he is able to establish the maximum amount of communication with a horse.

I think there is a whole myriad of abuses in the horse industry. Not abuses where people tie up a horse and don't feed or water it, or beat the horse. I'm talking about abuse from standpoint of just not understanding at all what this horse is about—how the horse thinks. Horses by nature want to get along and want to please, but when people treat their horses like pieces of machinery, the people lose so much.

We watch horse babies as they're learning—in their playtime and as they eat and sleep. We not only can tell a lot about what they might be as future performance prospects and about their minds, but also teach ourselves a lot about horses. No one ever lives long enough to have a complete mastery and understanding of horses, but if we don't start the journey, we miss much of the enjoyment we can have from horses.

I love the recreational part of riding a 2-year-old. I always look forward to the first time I ride one down the road on our place and all of a sudden he sees that big trailer bed we use for a culvert. He's never seen anything like that before. Sitting on him, I look forward to seeing how he reacts because that tells me some things about this colt.

Eighty percent of riders might slap that colt with the reins and force him to go up to the scary thing. Are these riders teaching their horses they are going to be punished when something is frightening?

I wait to see if my colt turns around and wants to run, or if he wants to investigate, or maybe step closer to that scary thing. That situation is neat to me. If a 2-year-old has never seen something like that and just goes plodding across it, I'd just want to take off the saddle and carry it back to the barn myself. I'd think, "This is a dumb son of a gun!"

I don't want my horse to be a robot! I want my horse to be my partner. I'm the partner who makes the decisions, but in everything I do with the horse, I want him to hold up his end of the bargain. The only way he becomes that willing partner is if I listen to his part of the conversation—even when I'm leading the conversation.

Some people who think they're great riders don't realize that they're only talking—and seldom listening to their horses.

My horse is telling me something all the time—and I can be a good boss or a bad boss. I don't want to get my horse so totally trained that he walks over a cliff or steps on a rattlesnake because I tell him so. I want him to have the confidence to say, "Hey there's a rattlesnake here!" and know that I listen to him. The horse's part of the conversation can be huge—and I want to hear what he's telling me. I don't think it's in a horse's nature to fake things.

In writing this book, it is not the intention to teach solely how to train a finished reining horse or how to be show-ready. Instead I use the reining maneuvers to show the reader how to listen to the horse. The reader can use my set of basics not only to achieve a well-trained, soft, supple, responsive horse, but also, hopefully, to adapt these same basics to training a rope horse, a cutting horse, a polo pony, or perhaps a quiet, responsive trail-riding horse.

My entire purpose has been to utilize the basics to increase your knowledge in such a way that the door swings open for you to train your horse with understanding and empathy. Perhaps this can be my greatest contribution to the horse—the greatest creature on earth.

Dick Pieper

Section One

Creating the Language

To train a horse, you must first establish a means of communication—a language—that allows you, as the rider, and your horse to converse freely back and forth. The vernacular is physical, verbal and intuitive, but it is a distinct dialect that has been developed through years of trial and error.

As with any language, there are basics—rudiments of grammar and structure that must be learned first. With these primary tools, only the most elementary communication is possible, but the tools are the foundation for the entire language.

When these tools are properly built upon, a graduate-school level of learning is reached. The final product is limited only by your horse's physical abilities and your imagination.

"Pressure initiated by the trainer results in a correct response by the horse that is rewarded by the release of pressure by the trainer."

1

The Principles of Interaction

The horse's earliest survival depended on differentiation, or recognizing change, followed by a quick response. So we know that any kind of disturbance or outside pressure that interrupts a horse's comfort zone is going to cause him to take some sort of action.

The most effective training method takes this into consideration, building on one simple principle that is constant from the first day of human-equine interaction. The principle: Pressure initiated by the trainer results in a correct response by the horse that is rewarded by the release of pressure by the trainer.

Pressure

The pressure we're talking about is the pressure that comes from any action we take around the horse and from any of the various aids we use to give the horse direction. We use these aids—our hands, our legs, our body positions and our voices—to carry on our sides of the conversation in this special language we're creating.

If you learn a foreign language, you need a speaker to enunciate clearly and loudly. As you develop an "ear" for the unfamiliar sounds,

understanding is more natural. You begin to hear and understand subtle nuances and inflections—even whispered words.

In the same way, the more we converse with the horse, the more subtle our cues become. Ultimately, the cue might be a squeeze of the calf of the leg or the slightest movement of one bridle rein, or an almost imperceptible shifting of the rider's weight from one hipbone to another. Those cues can be invisible to a spectator but clearly understood by our horses. Why shout when we can whisper?

The Correct Response

Reaching that level of communication is entirely dependent on making the horse understand early that every cue is a request: "Please respond correctly to this pressure."

In the beginning the horse doesn't know what a correct response is. When he receives a cue, he just knows something feels different and he moves or reacts in some way. He might make several moves, but the rider continues the pressure until the horse makes the desired move.

When you learn to communicate your wishes, your horse learns to give the desired responses, such as flexing at the poll while loping in a given lead.

ROSS HECOX

The Reward

As soon as the horse does what the rider wants, he immediately releases the pressure. This says to the horse, "That's right, thanks."

By starting with one simple cue and repeating it over and over, several things happen.

First, the horse recognizes the cue as an attempt to communicate. Then he begins to understand that one specific response to that cue gets him a reward—the release from pressure. The more quickly the horse gives a correct response, the more quickly he gets the reward, the release.

Consistency in cueing your horse for poll flexion, for example, helps your horse figure out the desired response.
ROSS HECOX

When your horse responds well to your cue, you remove the cue—and the pressure on your horse to perform.
ROSS HECOX

So, the basis of our communication follows this pattern:

- The rider cues the horse.

- That horse responds correctly.

- The rider removes the cue.

To be effective, the rider has to cue the horse exactly the same way every time. Likewise, when the horse responds in the desired manner, the rider must stop the cue immediately and give the release.

The horse learns that when he feels a cue from the rider, there is a response that causes the cue to stop. Gradually the horse begins to respond automatically to a softer and lesser cue than previously given, and his response becomes more and more fine-tuned and subtle than before. As the cues become increasingly more sophisticated and the required skills become more difficult than they are at first, the horse stays confident because he always has been able eventually to give the correct response and cause the pressure to be released.

Training by this method takes into account the horse's mindset, instincts and natural reactions and replaces his natural tendencies with a stronger set of conditioned responses than he has initially.

Ultimately, we build the trust of the animal to the level that, even in insecure surroundings, he comes to rely on us for direction and security. Even when he is stressed, our familiar actions and cues reduce the stress. That is why a skilled trainer can take a green colt into a building with 5,000 spectators for the first time and expect him to perform. He knows he's developed the trust and response to the point that those things are stronger than the horse's fear of the unknown.

As the horse becomes more and more comfortable with giving those desired responses, the likelihood of his responses being interrupted by any sort of outside influence decreases substantially.

And that's the key to showing a horse. The horse's response to the rider becomes stronger than the horse's response to his surroundings.

Key Factors

How well the horse progresses in his training—by getting better at reading the rider's cues and learning responses that gain release

Conversational Courtesy

Keep in mind that it's a real conversation and communication you're having with this horse. Think of your conversations with other people.

Have you ever tried to talk with someone whose voice is so loud that you can't concentrate on what he says because of the irritating high volume? For a horse, that person is abrupt and harsh with his hands instead of smoothly applying pressure that increases gradually until there is a response. This rider cues harshly with no warning. He shouts to the horse—your goal is to communicate through whispers.

Then there's the person who forgets to release the cue—never gives the reward or says, "Thank you." Think of the person who asks you to do something that you quickly do, but soon that person asks you again without ever noticing that you already have done the job?

That's frustrating! Many riders unwittingly get that same frustrated response when they cue horses. The riders don't give the horses time to react before cueing again or cueing for something else.

Remember: The trainer is the boss, but to be effective, he must be considerate of the horse and his sensibilities. As an employee, you want consideration from your boss. Any worker wants to be able to expect fairness, consistency and good leadership from his superior.

So does your horse.

Conversational courtesy requires that you learn to communicate with your horse . . .
CANDICE NOYCE

. . . listen to his response . . .
CANDICE NOYCE

. . . and then say, "Thank you," with the release of pressure.
CANDICE NOYCE

from pressure—is almost entirely dependent upon three factors:

- The horse's mind is a critical factor, as is his willingness to accept training.

- The rider's consistency plays an important role as he gives the horse the same pressure to elicit the same response every single time a cue is given.

- The rider's ability to read the horse's response and react to it is equally important as the rider quickly and consistently releasing the pressure when the correct response is given.

When two people carry on a conversation, one asks a question or makes a statement.

The other person immediately answers. His answer elicits another response from the first person and so on. That's how a conversation is carried on.

Interacting with a horse is exactly the same kind of conversation.

In order to have this conversation with a horse and make it an active and continuous line of communication, we must be able to listen to the horse's side of the conversation and accurately read his responses. Then we can communicate back to him in a way that makes sense. Because humans are the ones with the ability to think and reason, we have to be the leaders in the conversation—and also the ones who understand and respond to the horse's side of the discourse.

Keep in mind that the horse's reaction to people always is the result of what you have

When your elbow is elevated and there is slight tension in your horse's neck, he must give his nose to the left in order to relieve the pressure from your cue.
ROSS HECOX

As your horse takes a second step along the path and figures out the desired response, your left elbow begins to soften and relax.
ROSS HECOX

done or what someone else has done in the past. If you react the same way every time, then one time lose your temper, kick him in the sides, jerk the reins or make any action that is different than the way you've been reacting in that situation, you immediately have created a two- or three-week setback.

The Correction

Remember: The severity of a correction must be in proportion to the severity of the offense. You must learn to read a wrong response accurately to correct it properly. There are three kinds of wrong responses.

- The horse just draws a blank and doesn't understand what you want him to do. In this case, you just continue the cue or repeat the cue.

With the third step, another crossover, your elbow relaxes and drops even more to release pressure and reward your horse.

ROSS HECOX

- The horse knows what you want him to do, but the response that you have gotten from him has not yet become consistent. In this case, you just reinforce the cue with a stronger leg or stronger hand or more exaggerated motion.

- The horse responds with blatant disobedience. If this is the case, you enforce the cue with as much pressure as it takes to get a response, but always make sure that as soon as a clear, correct response is given, you give a release from pressure. When the horse is blatantly disobeying, it is okay if you have to brace and pull with both hands as long as you still release immediately when he gives the response.

Too much punishment can be defined as using force, pressure or a severe reprimand after you have gained the correct response. That might happen this way: You ask the horse to move his body with your leg. No response. You continue to ask. This time he still doesn't move away from your leg but actually leans into you. Then you really ask with a lot of pressure and he just leans into you again. Now, your next move is to keep exerting the pressure, gradually engaging the spur and putting on as much pressure, steadily, as you can, until he finally moves away. The instant he moves away, your spurring has to cease. If you don't stop the pressure when the horse responds, it is too much punishment.

Nor does riding have a place for emotion in the process of interacting or carrying on this conversation with a horse. It makes no more sense to get angry at a horse than it does to get irritated at a rock.

There's also no place for excessive personification. Horses do not have the range of emotions that humans have.

You never want to punish the horse out of anger, but don't be afraid to correct a horse. Because he learns that an attitude of obedience and acceptance can allow him to get along, you save him from abuse later because he has learned the limits early.

Conversely, the more the horse is forced, the more his natural reactions, as far as fear and flight go, overcome the conditioned responses that you're trying to instill. When that happens, he's no longer able to react with

Your horse responds poorly to cues for one of three reasons—a lack of understanding, the lack of consistency, or disobedience.
ROSS HECOX

After you determine why your horse has given a wrong response and make an effective correction, your horse's next effort can be far better than his initial response.
ROSS HECOX

confidence. All he can do is to try, as quickly as possible, to avoid or stop the pain. A lot of training is done by force, using equipment or rider strength to muscle a horse into the desired behavior.

Forcing a horse to work doesn't teach a conditioned response—it instills an attitude of avoidance.

That skill of avoiding pain builds and grows just like the attitude of acceptance or cooperation in the other scenario. Like the horse that begins to respond more and more quickly to a cue, this horse learns how to better avoid the pain.

Eventually the horse that's trained through force becomes so good at avoidance that he can avoid 95 percent of what you're trying to do.

For example: The horse that has been taught to turn around, back up and change leads to avoid pain and force eventually becomes so good at avoidance that he avoids walking through the gate in the first place. Or he reverts to that natural flight instinct and "runs off" on a loose rein when he gets into the pen. The jumper does a U-turn before the jump; the rope horse refuses to go into the box; the Western pleasure horse begins to anticipate commands; and so on.

Positive Consistency

Every time we humans interact with a horse, we have either a positive or negative effect. Every time we walk into a stall to put halters on horses, we either make them both more comfortable and relaxed with our presence or we make them more apprehensive.

We must monitor our movements and behavior and demeanor—even as simple a thing as putting on a halter should be done exactly the same, with the same motions and the same quiet demeanor, each time.

Remember: It doesn't matter if the horse is young or old. Our presence either has a good or bad effect. Because of horse's nature, personality, and makeup, anything we do—especially with a horse that's young and green—is foreign to him and can cause some degree of apprehension. From the very beginning in a relationship with a horse, we want to channel this apprehension into a positive reaction that enables us to get the horse to do what we want.

The horse learns from interaction and repetition, and doesn't deduce and use logic in his learning process. Because of those things, each stage of learning he completes is progressive and provides the base for the next level.

If I ask a horse to give his head the first day and he lets me pull his head around, that's the correct response, so I release the pressure. After I have asked him many times to bend laterally, I expect him, as he feels the pressure, to softly give me his head. After about 90 days, I expect him to give me his head as soon as he feels the slack come out of the reins. All of those responses are correct responses at the time they are given.

In other words, I cannot expect the horse to know, the first time I pick up the rein, when the slack comes out that he should give his head. As he's able to understand more, I'm able to ask more than I did before. I just keep upping the ante and increasing the horse's level of finesse.

Once a learned pattern had been established through repetition, a horse does not

Consistency in riding your horse leads to established response patterns, no matter where you ride—in the pasture or in the pen, as shown in the chapter opening photo.
ROSS HECOX

have the ability to arbitrarily decide that he's not going to do the pattern that way. It's critical to understand that any refusal or reluctance is going to be a product of some other interrupting or outside factor—confusion, pain, fear, hunger or sex.

Horses do not plan not to do something or decide that they are not going to do a thing. In most cases, when an uninjured horse refuses to do something that he has been doing on a regular basis or fails to give the accustomed response, that is because the situation is inconsistent or the pressure-and-release that elicits the response in the first place has been inconsistently applied. In other words, the horse has become confused.

Successful horsemanship takes all our knowledge of the horse's abilities, mental capacities and natural tendencies. We must carefully control our interactions with him to reach the refined level of training that is our ultimate goal.

"... start with a colt that is athletic enough and talented enough to do the job, and never let him have a bad day."

2

What the Trainer Must Know

No one starts on a two-week trip without knowing his destination, but people often start riding horses with no idea of where they're going or what sort of direction they plan to take. When I train a reining futurity horse, I start him as a 2-year-old and try to have him ready to peak in December of his 3-year-old year so that he's ready for the National Reining Horse Association Futurity. That doesn't allow much time for mistakes.

The secret to success is start with a colt that is athletic enough and talented enough to do the job, and never let him have a bad day. I must stay aware, then be consistent. Eighteen months is not enough time for that horse to have a setback. Even so, I must use the horse's clock and not the calendar when charting his progress.

And that's the same for any horse whose future lies in any event.

Have a Plan

From the day he undertakes the project of schooling a 2-year-old, a trainer must have in his mind the entire chronological order for each step all the way to the finished product. And he must never deviate.

Change has an effect on the entire scope of the program. For example, a novice starts out with a 2-year-old. At first, everything seems to be going well, and then the novice runs into some problem. He talks to someone else who trains and decides to try that person's method.

So the novice changes the way he does things. That confuses the horse because this new method is based on a different background of basic training.

I don't imply that I never change methods. One of the most enjoyable things about training horses is that I continue to learn new methods. But when I change anything, it is with a lot of thought. I might decide to change something and work it into the next horse's training, but I don't change on the horse midstream. That's not fair to the horse. If I did that, I'd be saying that everything I taught him until now has been a lie.

If you are telling the horse, "I'm the leader," and then halfway through the program, say, "I don't know, let's try this," the horse is going to get confused and become increasingly inconsistent. In other words, if you're inconsistent with the horse, he mirrors that and becomes inconsistent with you.

This daughter of Playgun is a talented athlete, and I've tried my best to not ever let her have a bad day.

Consistency is part of my plan to help a horse understand the desired response to my cue. I must be consistent not only with my cue for lateral flexion shown here, but also with my release when the horse responds correctly.
ROSS HECOX

In this book, I outline a program that has complete continuity from beginning to end. Each step progresses naturally to the next and lays the foundation for more difficult tasks to come. The basic communications I use in the beginning are the same ones that I use later with the finished horse.

Workmanlike Willingness

In order for you to train a horse to a high performance level, you have to understand that the mental aspect is as important as or more important than the physical side. Before you can think of performing any physical maneuver with a horse, you have to develop that horse's willingness.

To do this, the trainer has to condition himself to remove any outside thoughts that might influence his work with the horse. He must train himself to ask for the same response and in the same way every time. His body language must be the same each time he asks for a particular maneuver.

Basics are important in both the physical and mental sense. In a horse's early training, the goal is to instill a set of basic skills. These are the building blocks on which every future maneuver is based. These are the controls that are used throughout his life. While he is learning those basic skills, the horse also learns an attitude of cooperation.

Just as he learns through a lot of repetition to respond correctly to pressure from the reins or the legs, the horse also learns to be acquiescent. I develop a sense of compliance in him. He learns through the repetition that I don't hurt him or overload his wagon, so he has nothing to fear. That sets the tone for our conversation.

I'm developing a workmanlike attitude in the horse—conditioning him to accept that most days he goes to the work area and does strenuous work for an hour to an hour and a half. He accepts this the same way he accepts the fact that I feed him, brush him or clean his stall daily.

How well a horse performs the second basic, for example, and softens through the poll relates directly to my focus while riding the horse.
ROSS HECOX

Consistency counts in developing a workmanlike attitude in a young horse, no matter the situation or the location.
ROSS HECOX

Reasoning or Repetition?

It is important to know how a horse learns. Understanding equine learning enables the horseman to communicate with a horse on a daily basis.

People reason—horses don't. People learn by generalization. Horses learn by differentiation and repetition.

A person might see a big green tractor in the north end of the pasture one day and investigate it to find that the large foreign object is not threatening. The next day, if the person goes into the pasture and the tractor is still there—but at the south end of the pasture—he probably would not bother to investigate; he learned the day before that the tractor is not harmful. The person also would reason that the tractor probably is the same one he investigated the day before.

For the horse, things work much differently.

First, when he is released into the pasture, he scans the area, looking for any changes that could mean potential danger. That tractor interrupts the familiar picture, and he responds by using his two natural defenses, quick reaction and flight. He snorts and runs away, but since he is confined to the area and can't leave, he might then carefully investigate every aspect of the pasture.

But even after investigating the tractor, and settling down, when the horse enters the pasture tomorrow and sees the same tractor in a different location, he most likely does not make the connection. To him, there is no connection between a change in the north end of the pasture and the tractor now in the south end. He's not going to "figure it out," or reason that is the same tractor. The horse notes the changed environment and reacts by being wary and careful because even a slight change in his surroundings could mean danger, just as it did to his wild ancestors.

A horse's memory of how his environment looks is remarkable and even the smallest differences are noticed and noted. Likewise, he is just as aware of his rider. Changes in the rider, his actions and his methods speak just as loudly.

Have you ever played the game in which someone brings out a tray of items and tells everyone to look at them? Then later, the same tray is displayed—minus one item to be identified. Not everyone does well at this game.

A horse could play this game in that he has the ability to differentiate—recognize changes in his environment—and that ability is developed to an amazing degree. But the horse cannot reason what the change is.

A horse learns through repetition and differentiation, not reasoning, but still comes to accept something that might be frightening at first as a routine part of his environment.
ROSS HECOX

Acceptance

I'm going to be able to establish this attitude of willingness and cooperation in almost every horse to a greater or lesser degree. But to be an outstanding reining horse— a futurity winner or world champion—it takes a horse that's willing to accept his work completely.

Some horses develop this attitude of acceptance only to a certain point. For example, maybe your reining horse can score a 70 or 71, but if you push him beyond that, he learns avoidance behaviors that make him difficult to control.

The length of time that it takes for a horse to develop this attitude of cooperation varies.

It can be a long time for some or a very short time for other horses.

A horse's physical capabilities have a bearing on his amount of acceptance. You might start a horse that, in the beginning, you think has a great mind. As he progresses and reaches the limits of his physical abilities, that's as far as his mind goes.

This horse is willing, but it's so hard for him physically because of his limited athletic ability. That shortcoming defeats him.

In the same way, sometimes that bionic equine athlete gets to the point that he says, "That's all I'm going to give you." That can happen even though you've brought him along slowly and done all the right things.

If you keep pushing, you lose. Your only option is to wait until the horse's mind can keep pace with his physical ability. Often that type horse can't be great as a young horse, but if you are able to wait, he might go on to be an outstanding older horse.

Like kids, some horses mature earlier and others later. Sometimes they mature mentally before their physical growth catches up or vice versa. It just depends on the individual.

Control Conditioning

I see the evidence of mental immaturity as resistance to the development of the willing attitude I'm after.

For example, I can be bringing a horse along slowly, asking for small progress, but I read signs that he's not gaining. He has great days and bad, easily can be distracted, is afraid to do a lot of things, and might be spooky, shy or silly.

The ideal is a physically capable horse that is mentally sound. He develops that willingness and workmanlike attitude at an early age. He's also strong enough physically so that the training process is not difficult for him. He's balanced and mature, and it's easy for him to work and do so willingly.

There are many outside factors that influence a horse's mental conditioning. Things like pain, hormonal distractions, nutrition imbalances—even being ridden too close to feeding time—can all have an effect on how the horse works.

You don't want to take a chance of having a bad ride because of such outside influences.

Try to control the situation so you don't have to compete with these factors. Never set the scenario for a confrontation. Avoid riding a sore horse. If the situation evolves to the point where the horse is sore and hates to see you coming, you're opening the door for him to learn all kinds of avoidance techniques and respond poorly.

It's important for the trainer to adjust his schedule to fit the horses. I ride the best horse first, the second best horse second, etc., and in the same order and time each day. I feel that this is the only way to be fair to the horse and to the customers.

With every step the horse takes, I'm looking for a sign that says I've asked too much. If I see such a sign, I back off and reassure. I retreat to a level on that maneuver that's below what the horse can do. Then I take a couple of days to build back up. I don't think anyone can train a horse to do anything unless that person is completely tuned into and striving to be aware of the horse.

Apprehension and Resistance

One key to success as a trainer is being able to tell the difference between apprehension and resistance. You have to deal with these two things in completely opposite ways.

The apprehension mode means, "Go back, relax, and reassure."

The resistance mode says, "Firmly encourage him to step right up and do whatever it is that you're asking him to do."

You, as the trainer, don't have all day to decide. The horse's attention span is so short that discipline must happen immediately. Discipline scares him only if it comes too late. Then the horse doesn't connect the discipline to the offense.

My whole system is based on that important pressure-response-release principle discussed in Chapter 1. These things relate to the mental as well as the physical aspects of performance:

- pressure from the rider
- correct response from the horse
- release from pressure by the rider

From the beginning, the thing I want to keep on the horse's mind is how to relieve himself of pressure. I apply pressure, and then the horse's job is to gain release. That never changes. From day one, in halter-breaking, he feels the pull. He reacts in a variety of ways, but he finally steps forward as desired. When he does, the pressure is released.

This horse's expression seems to be more apprehensive than resistant when being asked to perform basic number one.
ROSS HECOX

Here, the horse appears to be more resistant to, rather than apprehensive about, being cued for basic number two.
ROSS HECOX

In every situation, whether it is reining, leading, or any aspect of interaction with humans, the horse learns that he can gain a release from pressure. There's always a "right" response and he gains confidence in dealing with advances in his training because, as he confronts pressure, he expects to learn a correct response to release the pressure. In reining horses, this gaining release from pressure is highly defined. Ultimately, the great performer seeks a release from the suggestion of pressure.

It's so important that the horse should not perceive pressure as painful.

Always remember: The absolute error is failing to release the pressure when the horse responds correctly. That release makes all the difference in reducing the horse's apprehension and/or overcoming his resistance so he's willing to perform.

A thoughtful rider recognizes that tail-switching might come into play when initially teaching a young horse to move the hindquarters, basic number three.

ROSS HECOX

However, by taking a steady, consistent approach with the horse, a thoughtful rider also can develop a smooth canter departure—and without the horse's tail switching.

ROSS HECOX

Considerations for Success

As people begin and continue with their riding programs, a few things usually surface that have some bearing on success. Among them: consistent riding and personality and behavioral considerations.

Consistency. The key to success as a trainer is developing high degree of skill at being consistent. You become a great showman or rider by developing the kind of consistency with which you follow your program exactly, religiously and with no deviation.

The rider should have at least average timing and average balance. If the rider can be extremely consistent, the horse is the one that has to be the athlete.

Personality. A rider should learn which type of personality he gets along with best. Usually, a more aggressive rider needs a quieter, less sensitive horse. The more sensitive or quieter rider is going to get along with a more "feely" or explosive kind of horse.

Young trainers generally get along best in the beginning with really laid-back horses. As the trainers' skills and consistency, and knowledge of horses' minds improves, these young people become able to train a more sensitive and feely horse.

Behavior. There's always a cause when there is a behavior change in a horse. The wise trainer tries to recognize any factors that could result in behavior modification.

Recognizing Characteristics of a Horse's Mind

One time we bought a gorgeous Doc O'Lena mare in Canada. She had great conformation, and we thought she'd be a star.

She looked like an older mare, but had the mind of a yearling—easily distracted. She couldn't keep herself together and always was whinnying at other horses and looking at everything that was going on. She just wasn't mature enough to pay attention.

I could not get her to develop any willingness, so I couldn't ask her to do increasingly more difficult things.

I decided to put her on a holding pattern and wait until her mind caught up with her body. I ended up keeping her at about a mid-year level throughout her entire 3-year-old year, working her carefully, gradually asking for just tiny progress.

Finally, I began to see signs that she was making advances. When she was a 4-year-old, her mind caught up with her body. By the end of her 4-year-old year, she was a confident, willing performer.

Had she been spurred and pounded to make the futurity, she would have become a throwaway item. By going at her pace, we salvaged an outstanding individual.

The characteristics of Playgun's mind have been so desirable that he has become a top sire.

JOHN BRASSEAUX

It's a big mistake to start bestowing the horse with human tendencies. Even professional trainers can fall into the trap.

You hear, "He's just decided he doesn't want to do... " or "He needs to figure out this." A horse doesn't decide things or figure out things. His behavior is a reaction to the behavior of his trainer, his environment, his health, libido and conditioning. Since you know these things, your job as trainer is not to let outside influences affect the horse or yourself!

I know that I'm a morning person. I want to get up in the morning, have coffee and breakfast, and ride my futurity horses as early in the day as possible—before the phone calls, customer questions or business. I want to go to the barn with my mind uncluttered so I can focus on my horses and can devote my entire mental process to the goal of being consistent about how I do everything and how I ask for everything.

Sometimes I might have a horse at a critical stage, where I think I'm just about to make a breakthrough, or I feel that things are not going well with a horse. Maybe it's a day that started with a crisis and I'm behind schedule—or really rushed or out of sorts. I sometimes skip riding rather than ride in that instance; I'm in less than my optimum state of mind. I don't want to allow my morale to have a negative impact on my horse at a critical time in his development. My lack of being tuned into my horse could be detrimental. If I'm not at my best, I don't try to raise the degree of difficulty on any segment of training, but the only horse I actually skip is one at a critical stage.

Section Two

The Partner

In selecting a prospect, we take into consideration both a horse's physical and mental conformation. To be an athlete, he must be an exceptional individual. No matter what the event or job, he needs to have a body that is suited to his intended use.

The first selection decisions are based almost solely on conformation and breeding. We know that certain bloodlines and combinations of bloodlines have been very successful in the past and that conformation characteristics ensure that he's the athlete we want.

As the business of breeding performance horses has become more sophisticated, we know we can select a horse for inheritable characteristics. Probably the most dramatic illustration of heredity is mental attitude. It's amazing how many horses from the same family react alike. We get up in the morning and know what horses of that family are going to do.

After considering the breeding, we look at conformation and athleticism. Is the horse built to stay sound? Is he constructed so that it can be easy and natural for him to perform the maneuvers we're going to ask of him?

Finally, we want the horse to have had premium handling. We don't want him to have been exposed to any training or schooling that makes it hard for him to trust our program later.

3

Mental Conformation

Conformation refers to the outline or form of a horse—how the body is made. I believe there are two facets to the horse's makeup—the mental and the physical. The physical conformation I talk about in the next chapter tells me what kind of athlete a horse can be. The mental conformation tells me what kind of heart he might have, whether he is trustworthy, and if he can be mentally strong whether in a show arena or out on the trail.

Genetics

I think that genetics play a great part in both the mental and the physical aspects of a horse. First, when considering a young prospect, I know the genetics tell me what mental traits the horse has or how this horse reacts to different stimuli because his relatives react in the same ways.

Here's an example. All the foals by our stallion Playgun have this trait. If riders are rough training them, the horses become very fearful and are liable to react the wrong way because they're afraid. They might be faced up to a cow and jump in the wrong direction; they're afraid if they don't move the right way, their riders might get after them. The horses put enough pressure on themselves. If the riders try to put too much more pressure on these horses, they overreact. But when riders are fair to these horses and correct them without overdoing things, they're great to ride.

The point: Different bloodlines react differently to training. The further you go as a rider or trainer, the more you recognize different traits in horses by a specific stallion. For example, the Doc's Hickory horses could be very reactive, extremely cowy and were terrific overachievers. They had to be quieted down and constantly reassured with a lot of slow, methodical repetition. The Doc Quixote horses were a little different in that they were very calm, good-minded horses and still very cowy, but much more laid-back. At times you needed to speed them up, as opposed to the Hickorys, which you always were trying to slow down. These two extreme opposites illustrate the differences in mental conformation.

Once you've considered the sire, consider the traits of the dam, based on her breeding. With those two criteria you can, with a fair degree of accuracy, predict how their young horses are going to train. You should pay attention to these things and catalog them in memory in your quest to become a horseman. Study each horse you ride and eventually you

---

A horse with a great body might perform well athletically, but a horse with a great body and a strong mind has the heart to deliver more than sometimes seems physically possible, as Playgun demonstrates here.

The more you learn about a foal's bloodlines, the better you're clued in to how that horse might respond to training when the time comes.

DARRELL DODDS

Genetics can be an important consideration when evaluating a horse for a particular purpose.

ROSS HECOX

see the similarities in horses bred along the same lines. This type knowledge helps you know how to mold a horse and give him confidence.

I rode Miss Cee Blair, owned by the Rae B. Williams, Raleigh, N.C., to a top-five finish in the National Reining Horse Association Futurity. The mare had babies for five years and was purchased by Roland Beeson and Bob Kidd. Then the partnership sent the mare and a full sister, Cee Blair Masota, whom I rode to a co-reserve championship in the futurity, to Willowbrook Farms in Catasauqua, Penn., to breed to Corona Cody. I was training there at the time. The owners said, kind of in a kidding way, for me to ride both mares and that I could keep and show whichever I thought could do the best.

Early in the year I picked Miss Cee Blair. The first time I showed her, I won an NRHA open reining and, encouraged by that, I took her to another and won again. Being that

What I learned about Miss Cee Blair, an outstanding reining horse in both her youth and her maturity, later helped me successfully compete on her sisters, brothers and eventually her son, Cee Blair Sailor.

TOM FULLER, COURTESY DICK AND BRENDA PIEPER

successful early in the year, I thought there was a possibility I could show her to a world championship in the open division. After a phone call to Beeson and Kid, I started hauling the mare in earnest. At the end of that year, she had won more money than any other open horse had ever won in a single year and was the NRHA open world champion. Her record in earnings held for almost 10 years until finally broken by Cee Blair Sailor, her son. I also rode three of Miss Cee Blair's full brothers and sisters. By the time I got to the second or third one, I knew what those horses would do in training each day before I walked out of the house.

You do not learn this information from a book. But if you are aware and pay attention, these things become more clear to you at an earlier stage in your development as a horseman.

With that said, the horse's mental conformation also can be affected by his early handling and then ultimately by his training or the lack of it.

What you're looking at in this chapter essentially arc outward responses and actions that tell you how a horse responds to training. You also come to know fairly early to what level of training you can take him, whether it's to the very top futurity level, or to a weekend, non-pro or other level of expertise. Any time you're training horses, you find that a horse is comfortable within his level of ability, but once pushed past that, he becomes uncomfortable and is apt to make both physical and mental mistakes.

Use genetics as a factor to evaluate a prospect for your intended use. Make sure he comes from families, top and bottom, that consistently produce horses that can do what you want a horse to do.

Pasture Evaluation

My guidelines below are for the type of horse I've found to be the most trainable and the most able to excel in any range of use, from the very top show horse to the very best recreational horse.

First of all in the selection process, I look for a prospect that's a happy-acting horse. Whether I approach him in a pasture, pen or stall, I don't want him to pin his ears or have a bad attitude; that type of response only gives me a negative impression of the horse. I've found that the horse that seems to be in a good mood and happy most of the time is able to become comfortable in almost any situation I put him.

When I walk with a normal, nonthreatening posture toward a group of yearlings in a pasture, I'm not going to go directly to any one horse. I just walk out there slowly and watch to see how the yearlings react to me and to the other horses. I'm very nonconfrontational but I closely observe how the young horses react. In a typical group I see very different personalities. Some appear to be curious, let me approach them or even step up to me with their ears up. Other horses try to get away; their eyes are big and maybe their tails are up. They want to run away and try to get the other horses to leave with them. Then there's the aggressive horse that strides right up and tries to be my boss.

I watch how the horses respond to me and also watch how they interact with each other. When I look at horses in a group, I'm probably not there to look at the herd boss—the one chasing everyone else away from that feeder. I'm also not looking for the most timid individual in the bunch, the one that gets chased away from the feed.

Every time I ride through my pasture, I evaluate the horses I see—how each responds to the others, as well as to my riding horse and me.

DARRELL DODDS

The boss horse often has a temper and can be a overly aggressive in kicking and biting other horses, running them away from feed, and just being extremely bossy. As trainer, establishing myself over him in the pecking order might be harder than it is with a horse that isn't the herd leader. The herd boss wants to treat and respond to me the same way he does to other horses—fighting back, trying to be boss. The herd leader is mentally bolder and more aggressive than other horses. Trying to train that horse mentally to do exactly what I want and when I want can lead to confrontations with him.

I'm always after the horse in the middle of the pecking order, the one that has his ears up and seems a little curious. He might be timid but he's not afraid. In my experience, that translates to the kind of horse that almost enjoys or looks forward to the training process—as long as he is treated fairly, corrected when necessary and praised when needed. This kind of horse has almost no limits mentally to the level I could take him.

I don't want to consider a horse that's really afraid and timid. When I approach, that's the one who wants to turn and run to the other end of the pasture, and stay there. When it comes to training this horse, he generally is sweet and easy to teach, but often can be gutless when it's time to step up and perform. He might be afraid of a little piece of paper on the ground, to cross the water or step over a log. When I take him into that arena, he's scared of shadows and on the trail he finds a lot to fear. In the show pen, maybe the ground doesn't suit him or he's a little tired, so he just gives up. Or maybe the announcer's stand looks spooky, so he's afraid to go near it.

I've found that, later in training, I can improve this horse's confidence to a certain extent; he gets better as he learns to trust me more. But when in a different situation, one he's not comfortable with or doesn't understand, he probably always reverts to flight as a solution. In the pasture he's afraid of those other horses, easily pushed away from the feed and easily intimidated, and possibly those other horses pick on this timid one.

You can overcome a lot of these obstacles by training. But you can't overcome all of them to the point that a timid horse becomes a total top-shelf horse you can put in any situation and trust.

Ultimately I want a horse that makes an effort, whether on the trail, in the show ring or working cattle. If I ride him up to a vertical wall, he says, "I don't know, boss. It looks tough to me but I'll try it for you." That's the horse I want to develop and that timid horse doesn't always get there. Certainly during the training process, I make him better, more confident and fairly dependable, but he's never as good as the horse with that unafraid mental outlook.

Selecting a prospect, based on his mental outlook, comes down to whether the horse is gutless or gritty. The gutless horse has been fearful and nervous all his life. Even though you modify his behavior with training, under extreme stress he reverts to his original mindset. The horse that is curious about you and life in general, a little careful but not totally afraid, is your ideal. His curiosity and interest overcome his fear and he wants to know what you're about. This horse, in the final analysis, can be the gritty horse that is always there for you—solid in every situation.

Personality Traits

The horse's personality develops from the combination of his genetic tendencies and his life experiences, the training and handling he receives throughout his life. A horse's personality can be molded by schooling or conditioning, but the raw material is in the horse's genetics when you start your training program. Those inherited characteristics affect your program results. That's why bloodlines have become so important in the horse industry.

Geldings Can Last a Long Time

For a good example of a gelding's longevity, look at the indomitable King Cactus Bill. I originally trained the gelding from 1983 to 1991, then horse carried a variety of youth and non-pro riders to successful show-ring appearances in National Reining Horse Association, as well as American Quarter Horse Association competition. Todd Refitt, Keater Prevatt, Barbara Gerken, Lyn Johnson, Ann Melvin, Ivy Lea Pohlman and Sarah Johnson all earned money and points on King Cactus Bill in the reining pen.

The raw material for personality is in a young horse's genes, but training can help mold and shape it.

BRENDA PIEPER

Texas Kicker's level-headed style of stopping was part of his genetic make-up, so I tried not to get in the way of that when training him.

CHERYL CODY

Enduring Excellence

Cee Blair Sailor was the youngest stallion to be inducted into the National Reining Horse Association Hall of Fame—and with good reason. After training "Sailor" I rode him to a top 10 placing in the 1991 NRHA Futurity, the 1992 Lazy E Classic, and at other major shows.

David and Carmel Connor owned Sailor. Their daughter, Amanda, began to show Sailor in 1993, placing an incredible 36 times on her way to a NRHA intermediate non-pro world title. This division is for non-professional riders who have not yet earned their way into the top non-pro division. Non-pro competition generally is less competitive than the open division, so it was almost unbelievable when this equine athlete came back in 1994 with trainer Craig Schmersal.

Sailor immediately went back to the very top, placing 89 times in the toughest open competition! Amazingly, only two of those placings were below second place. Not surprisingly, Sailor added two more world titles—the open and limited-open championships—to his credit that year.

Cee Blair Sailor had all the ingredients to make an outstanding athlete. His dam, Miss Cee Blair, had been a reining futurity finalist for me in 1980, when the event was held during the All American Quarter Horse Congress in Columbus, Ohio, and in 1985 she won the NRHA open world championship.

Cee Blair Sailor, the youngest stallion inducted into the National Reining Horse Association Hall of Fame, was Miss Cee Blair's son, and my experience with her proved beneficial years later when riding him.

HAROLD CAMPTON PHOTOGRAPHY

In our Pieper Ranch breeding program, my wife and I have been very careful to select bloodlines that we feel have strong mental characteristics that enhance the type of horses we're interested in producing. Our horse's genetic bloodlines come largely from the cutting and reining worlds. However, these also are the kind of bloodlines that fit well throughout the spectrum of all Western horse disciplines, as well as for both amateur and recreational riders.

Texas Kicker, for example, is a son of Colonel Freckles. Colonel Freckles was a beautiful horse with nearly perfect physical conformation. He also had a quiet mind, and was a very docile, trainable kind of horse. He had won the National Cutting Horse Association Futurity but also was very suitable for many disciplines, including reining, Western pleasure, Western riding and roping, and he also sired wonderful recreational horses. He probably was on of the most popular sires of the 1980s and '90s.

Texas Kicker's mother was by Mister Gold 95, a son of Hollywood Gold, owned by the Four Sixes Ranch of Guthrie, Texas. Many mares the ranch owns to this day trace back to Hollywood Gold. Mr Gold 95's daughter, Miss Ginger Dee, was co-champion of the NCHA Futurity. Even though many of Hollywood Gold's foals have been great performers, they also have been great ranch horses popular throughout the West.

These are the kinds of bloodlines that we feel are so important. These bloodlines have the ability to achieve our goal of producing all-around good horses that perform well in almost any discipline.

Our second stallion, Playgun, was a son of Freckles Playboy, a three-quarter brother to Colonel Freckles. Playgun's dam was a daughter of Doc's Hickory. Playgun was champion of both open and non-pro Augusta Cutting Horse Futurities and went on to win $184,000 in NCHA Competition. He remains number eight on the list of all-time leading sires of cutting horses and his get have won well over $7 million in the cutting arena. However, Playgun's greatest contribution has been as a sire of roping and ranch horses. A great many ranches have sons of Playgun to breed ranch mares because those sires enable the ranches to produce superior working and roping horses.

The stallion, Real Gun, once owned by the Stuart Ranch of Waurika, Okla., was the 2004 American Quarter Horse Association Superhorse, being shown in reining, working cow horse, calf roping, heading and heeling. Although Real Gun has been a fabulous arena horse, his get are now the foundation of Stuart Ranch's using-horse program and daily work any task required on the ranch.

So many times horses that excel in the show ring have offspring that quite often become the same good-minded, quiet, compliant horses that are perfect for everyday ranch work or recreational riding. It's important to realize, though, that you can start with a great horse mentally, but give him the wrong interaction and training, and cause the horse to become defensive and unreliable, overcoming his genetic makeup.

Physical Clues to Mental Outlook

When I have a horse that looks similar to another I've had, I usually find similarities in the horses' mental makeup and attitudes. Through the years, I've also found that certain appearances, points in physical conformation, seem to indicate distinct traits and give me insights into the horses' personalities. These personality traits almost are reflected in the looks of their faces. Of course, there are exceptions, but these personality tendencies, I've noticed, have been consistent with certain physical traits.

- A pig-eyed horse, for example, usually is stubborn. This is that type of passive-aggressive horse reluctant to do whatever you'd like him to do. In some cases you can get through to the horse and get him to do some elementary things, but he's not going to be your best horse.

- Floppy, relaxed ears usually translate to an even disposition. This is the patient horse that doesn't get easily stressed or upset about things.

- Little ears that stick up and hook in can indicate a temper. I've had a lot of horses with these ears through the years and they can be good horses, but they seem to be able to get mad easier than many horses.

- A Roman nose and/or a thick, coarse muzzle tell me that a horse can be stiff and dull—slow to react. Usually this horse isn't your brightest pupil that "gets" it every time you introduce something. Instead, he takes a lot more reinforcement and repetition on each step.

Also, because of their breeding, some horses are just more prone to have attitudes of acceptance than do other horses. Acceptance is a strong genetic trait, which that can be enhanced by good handling and careful training.

The opposite is the horse that becomes stressed in the most normal day-to-day situations. He's timid, insecure, and very susceptible to outside influences. Maybe he gets upset if you move a horse he likes to another pasture or stall, calling for his friend and pacing incessantly. He spooks if you park the horse trailer in a different place and he jumps at shadows. Again, although this type horse certainly can be trained and developed, he's not going to be in the top echelon even if he is made to become the best he can be.

Handling Stress

The horse's ability to handle stress is a very important aspect of his mental makeup. A horse's mental outlook can make him more or less susceptible to developing problems when he is subjected to stress—from weaning to training to hauling to showing. The horse I've been describing as desirable is one that, in my experience, can handle the stress of his environment, whatever that might be.

If a horse isn't strong mentally, stress can result in a variety of responses, from such vices, such as cribbing or weaving to biting, kicking or pawing. There are also health issues, such as a stressed horse not eating his total grain ration so he isn't able to remain fit. A horse susceptible to stress also is a candidate for ulcers and other conditions that are exacerbated by stress. The less susceptible a horse is to stress, the better performer he can make.

Helping horses deal well with anxiety is important, so I try to work with them from the beginning to expose each horse to potentially stress-causing situations, but in a controlled environment. As a trainer, I like to ride my horses in as many different environments and situations as I can. From riding a horse across creeks and over logs to having him go by a loud tractor, I want to give each horse confidence and reassurance. I also haul 3-year-olds along with another older, seasoned horse to shows. I unload and ride those youngsters while waiting for a class. The young horses can get acclimated to the hustle and bustle of the show environment while under no pressure to perform, and this also gives me a chance to evaluate each horse's reactions. I see which horses take the trip in stride and which ones react negatively. If a horse can't seem to cope mentally with an afternoon at a small Texas show, for example, he's not an All American Quarter Horse Congress futurity candidate.

As for sex, I think stallions are stronger, tougher and a little grittier than other horses. Stallions can take rigors of hauling and being in different environments, and have more staying power than many horses. A good-tempered, nice-minded stallion is the most ideal performing horse to me; however, stallions like this are few and far between.

I love a good mare that is even-tempered day in and day out. I do not believe the many negative things said about mares. My personal experience with mares is that I just ride them day in and day out; I don't pay much attention to their estrus cycles and this seems to work out well for me.

Probably overall, geldings are the most even-tempered, compliant and willing horses, and they often able to perform well for many years. For the average horse owner who isn't interested in building a breeding program, geldings are the best bet.

Hauling horses and riding them in various places not only gives them new experiences, but also allows me an amount of control to help minimize stress.
DARRELL DODDS

"Overall balance is the key to a well-built horse."

4

Physical Conformation

In a performance horse, everything relates to soundness and movement, so I want to avoid any conformation that causes movement for a horse's chosen use to be less than ideal. If I'm looking at an expensive prospect, I want the horse to be as near perfect physically as possible. In assessing him, I'm trying to predict the horse's ability to perform, so I look for physical traits that I know translate to solid performance and longevity. Soundness is a key issue, no matter the horse's intended use. Obviously anyone wants a long career for a show horse and likewise for a recreational horse that can be enjoyed for a long, long time.

The Prepurchase Exam

Even though a horse looks great, a prepurchase check for soundness by a knowledgeable veterinarian is a must for any horse I might purchase, and I ask for an extensive examination. In a 2-year-old prospect with a limited amount of riding, it's unlikely to see significant radiographic changes on X-rays, which could indicate a problem. For this reason, a flex test might be a better diagnostic test than X-rays for a horse of this age. Later, as a horse has been used and has experienced more physical stress, radiographs can be of greater significance than a flex test.

To flex-test a horse, the animal's leg is held in a flexed position for 30 seconds to a minute and then the horse is trotted immediately, and the gait analyzed for abnormalities and unevenness. The flexion places stress on the joint capsule and soft tissue, as well as the cartilage and bone, usually accentuating any lameness that is present.

If the horse represents a substantial investment, I likely ask for a complete set of radiographs—including knees, ankles and hocks—to rule out the presence of OCD, or osteochondritis dissecans. Osteochondritis is a failure of the subchondral bone, underneath the smooth articular cartilage inside the joints, to form properly from the skeleton's cartilage template. This weakness results in cracking and fissure formation in the articular cartilage when the foal, yearling or young horse bears weight on joints during exercise. Often the horse with OCD has shown no sign of lameness in the past but a veterinarian can give his opinion and prognosis for usability.

A horse's performance should help me make the decision that he becomes a breeding animal or not. If I plan to buy a stallion, possibly for breeding later, I also might include a breeding-soundness evaluation by the veterinarian that might include a check of the testicles and a semen test. In the case of a filly, a veterinarian might palpate to evaluate.

Find the Balance

When considering a young prospect, often you are trying to get an idea of what the horse might look like as an adult. Horses go through phases and

In looking at a horse's conformation, I want to see physical characteristics that contribute to solid performance and a long career.

ROSS HECOXI

often look quite different at various stages of youth. You have to learn how to look at a weanling, a yearling or a 2-year-old differently than you do a mature horse. Your eye must be developed and educated to assess young horses at these different ages and stages of development. That's where conformation comes into the picture.

Overall balance is the key to a well-built horse of any age, and learning to look at the overall picture is the first step for anyone who's trying to learn about conformation. The individual parts of a horse—straight legs, good back, powerful hindquarters, etc.—all can be there, but if the horse's build isn't balanced, the horse still might look like he has been made by a committee.

So look for a horse in which everything fits together. His neck is not too long for his body; his rear is not too massive in comparison to the rest of his body, and he isn't too leggy. Balance creates an overall pretty picture. All the horse's body parts are in proportion and that also equals a balanced and pretty mover.

When learning to look at conformation, there's a tendency to look at the parts, and you must do that to learn, but eventually you also must look at the entire horse with an eye that you've developed by looking critically at hundreds and thousands of horses. Being able to evaluate conformation is a skill that takes a lot of work.

Get a Visual

In the beginning, to make studying a horse's build easy, you might evaluate conformation by visually cutting the horse in half horizontally. The top half is from his belly up through the top line, and the bottom half is from his belly down to the ground. So if you say you're looking at the top of a horse, you're looking up from the horse's belly.

When I next look at a horse, my eyes then go from the top down. I look for problems below that horizontal line, but if the top line and balance are incorrect, I don't bother to look further. The reason: The upper flaws in conformation affect the horse's ability to move, stop, turn around and maneuver. Only

A key factor in recognizing a well-built horse is learning to recognize overall balance in a horse's conformation.
BRENDA PIEPER

After looking for overall balance in conformation, imagine a dotted line running horizontally through the horse's body and evaluate the top half and then the bottom half.

BRENDA PIEPER

after a horse has been found satisfactory above that dividing line, do I look below to see if the horse can stay sound for the level and intensity of maneuvers that his upper body allows.

That top line is so important! To see it clearly, move away from the horse, about 15 feet to the side. When looking at a horse from a position perpendicular to his middle, it's ideal, for example, that the highest point of the withers and the highest points of the hips are as close to even with one another as possible. Keep in mind that a young horse can have a growth spurt that leaves the hips higher than they ultimately are, but even a yearling with substantially high hips should be discredited.

A horse that appears a little low in the front end is not that bad, but that low front end becomes increasingly significant as the length of the back increases. In other words, the combination of a long back, low withers and a high hip is unacceptable.

The Upper Half

Here's an overview of what I consider when I look above that imaginary line dividing a horse horizontally.

Neck. If the hip and withers are in balance and the back is acceptable, I look next at the horse's neck. The ratio of the top line of that neck as compared with the underline of the horse's neck is a good starting point.

I like the neck long from the poll to the withers, and short from the throatlatch to where the neck ties into the shoulders. The longer the top line, as compared to the length of the underline, the better. In other words, when the top line is longer than underneath the neck, the better the horse's head hangs on his neck for him to easily give in the poll; in the extreme, the horse could carry his head perfectly collected all the time.

The fact that a horse's head hangs as closely to the ideal as possible doesn't replace training, but can make it easy for that horse to do what you want simply because the horse

The neck is an important area to consider because physical components there directly affect how easily a horse can perform certain maneuvers.

ROSS HECOXI

doesn't have to work against his conformation. In teaching collection, it is much easier to stretch a horse's top line and develop muscles over the neck, back and hip to support collection when the horse's neck is ideal.

With a heavy neck, a horse's mobility is impaired, and if he wants, that horse has the strength to be rigid and resistant. The build of the neck also can affect the horse's balance point. If he's heavy-necked, he is somewhat front-end heavy when you try to teach him maneuvers.

A neck that's too long and too limber also makes it difficult to get a horse's body to follow and perform well. That individual has a tendency to be a little bit off-balance at times. When a horse is too limber, it's easy for him to give you his head while his body just goes off in another direction.

Watch the horse's neck as he travels. You can be fooled by looking at the horse when he's only in the stall. Watch him move outside, travel and react. If his head is in the air all the time and his back is hollow, pass on the horse. You want a prospect to travel comfortably with his neck out front and to be most comfortable when his poll is level with his withers.

Look for a nice, clean throatlatch, too. A horse with a big, heavy gristly throatlatch tends not to be soft and supple through the poll.

Eye. When considering a prospect, the eye is important. You can tell about mind and disposition by the appearance of a horse's eye. The ideal is a big, round, pretty, kind-looking eye that sits out and on the sides of the head a little bit, so that the horse has good peripheral vision.

Muzzle and jaw. I prefer a fine, nice muzzle and look for fairly clean lines underneath the jaws. The ideal horse is somewhat flat along the sides of the jaw. I always have liked riding my horses in a hackamore at some stages. A horse with a clean throatlatch and flat sides of the jaws seems much more responsive in the hackamore than a horse that don't have those traits.

Head. When selecting a prospect, look for a generally pretty head. You've heard, "Horses don't have to be pretty to be good." Well, in the big league, they do. You want an attractive eye-pleasing horse that gives such an appearance, when he walks into the arena, that people hope he does well because he makes that strong, good impression. A pretty head goes a long way toward accomplishing that.

A horse with a clean throatlatch and flat-sided jaws seems more responsive to a hackamore than a horse without those characteristics.

ROSS HECOXI

Tail-set. I like a fairly low tail-set on a horse. That's something basically cosmetic, but the cosmetic is big part of presentation. Then, too, I usually see this physical characteristic with a long sloping croup. In a horse with a high tail-set, I usually see a flat croup and hocks that extend behind.

Wither. Look for a clean wither, one that is not meaty, thick or heavy because such a horse is predisposed to soreness; the saddle hurts his back. Seldom does a high-withered horse have fat withers. Usually the low-withered horses have that problem.

I don't rule out a high-withered horse that's also thin and narrow as a prospect, but I am aware that he might be hard to fit with saddle and might need other special equipment. So, all things being equal, this conformation is a negative.

Ribs. I want to see a horse with well-sprung ribs and an average length back, rather than a slab-sided or flat-sided horse. If a horse has well-sprung ribs and a strong belly, and the angles are correct on the ends, he also has a long underline.

The Lower Half

Now move to the lower half of the horse, evaluating this area in the same, precise manner you used before.

Shoulder. Looking at the shoulder of the horse, it's important to understand that in reining and cutting, the ideal in the shoulders and front-end conformation is to have exceptional mobility and lateral reach. Remember, the shoulder is the only joint in the front end that rotates laterally.

The ability to flex the joints easily and without pain is essential to a horse's soundness and soft movement. The more flexibility the horse has in front, the easier it is for him to perform reining, cutting and cow-horse maneuvers.

I want a horse with a sloping, medium shoulder rather than a long shoulder. Where I want length is in the humerus, a long humerus that slopes back from the shoulder. Then, when I look from the side, I can see that this positions the elbow well under the horse's body.

The joint connecting the shoulder and humerus should be placed high, and I can look at the joint and see if it is placed desirably. What I can't see—until I see the horse move—is the degree of rotation he has. There can be from three to five degrees of rotational difference from one horse to another.

The greater the rotation, the greater the horse's lateral reach can be.

Forearm and cannon. I want a horse to have a long forearm and short cannon. The more the ratio of forearm to cannon increases, the flatter the knee and the prettier the galloping action is. Conversely, the shorter the forearm and the longer the cannon, the more knee action a horse displays.

A happy medium is ideal for a reiner or cutter, but either extreme can be problematic. Although an extremely flat-kneed mover presents a soft, beautiful and pleasing picture at a lope, the horse can look stiff-kneed when stopping. The other extreme, a horse with a lot of knee action, has a choppy look when the horse lopes in the circle, but that active front end stays soft and loose when stopping.

So I'm looking for a compromise of pleasing movement when the horse travels in those circles and a rhythmic pedaling action in the front end during the stops.

Pastern. The pastern joint is a shock absorber. The pastern must be medium in length with a medium angle.

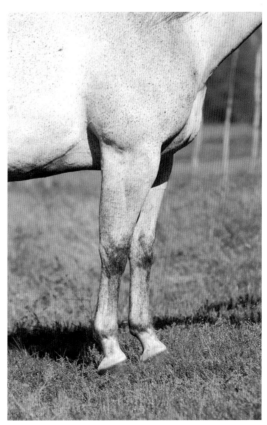

A structurally correct horse can perform athletically and with less risk of injury, so often has a long career.
ROSS HECOX

Long, lower-angled pasterns have too much give, or hyperflexion. A horse with this type of conformation, when subjected to hard work, is susceptible to bowed tendons, suspensory ligament strains, and check ligament problems. In addition, because a long, sloping pastern places the hoof in front of the leg column, such a horse has a tendency to step on himself while spinning, and often tips his shoulder to the inside to compensate.

If these problems are not enough, the hyperflexion at high speeds causes the hoof to the leave the ground late and out of sync. This, in turn, causes a hind shoe to catch a front one, bending the shoe or tearing it off the hoof completely. When a hoof is directly underneath the leg column, the horse lands smoothly and breaks over quickly.

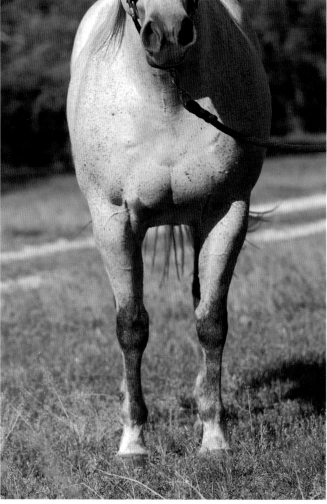

Straight columns of bones and sound feet contribute to a serviceable riding horse for the long-term; any structural deviation eventually stresses a horse's joints and likely can shorten his career.

ROSS HECOX

A horse with excessively short pasterns can be rougher moving and have less shock-absorption than a horse with medium pasterns. Not only does the short-pasterned horse's movement feel rough to the rider, the horse can't absorb enough shock from pounding the ground to prevent concussion-related stress. A horse with a short pastern also tends to develop ringbone and other concussion- related problems.

Leg column. From the front, look at the horse's leg columns from the shoulder down. Both front feet should point straight forward. Look to see that the knee, ankle and foot are in a straight column. Any deviation outward or inward causes stress to the joints and ultimately can mean arthritic conditions and calcification, or hardening of the structures.

When a horse toes in or out, the worst downside is that the horse's foot does not land flat. If he toes out, he lands on the inside of his foot; if he toes in, the outside of his foot hits the ground first. Either deviation increases the likelihood of excessive strain that might cause the horse's structure to break down, especially under hard work as a 3-year-old.

While still looking at the horse's front end, it is very important to note that a prospect's front legs come directly out of the centers of his shoulders. If a front leg comes out of the shoulder to the outside, the horse is a poor mover; if the leg comes from the inside of the shoulder, the horse interferes or hits his legs together.

It is a very common misconception that a horse with a wide front end can't turn around. Actually, several factors examined a little later help determine if that's the case. Remember, a horse can be wide across the chest as long as his legs come out of the centers of the shoulders and aren't parked clear out on the corners. If the legs come from the centers of wide shoulders, that's ideal.

Blemishes. While looking at a horse, note any blemishes, such as splints or scars. Cause is important here. If a blemish appears because it seems as if a horse can't hold up to regular work, that's a concern. But if the horse has a little scar that is likely the result of an accident, you probably can overlook that unless the blemish is large enough to affect the horse's later marketability.

Knee. I look for a broad, flat knee, one that has an appearance of size and strength. Some horses have offset knees, where the cannon doesn't come out of the center of the knee, so there is uneven pressure as the horse is worked and that translates to spurs or chips in the knee.

Think of the leg as a somewhat rectangular box, but with one end of the box smaller than the other. On that flat end surface, the box stands true. However, if the box seems to tilt, like it's standing on one corner, that indicates a problem in the knee alignment.

The joints of the knee act as shock absorbers and if the horse's build is correct, the concussion from his movement is spread evenly throughout the entire knee. When a horse has a crooked knee, where the joints are tilted, shock-absorption takes place on a small surface, causing extreme pressure in one area. Soreness can result and a chip in the knee might also develop.

Ankle. If the knee surface is a rectangle, then the front view of the ankle might be likened to a ball that should be centered under the cannon. From the side, the shape of the ball should not be pronounced at the front. The less bulge there, the better. On a yearling, a large bulge on the surface of the ankle means that he's already stressing this area, just from running and playing, and this is a weak part of his structure.

Feet. A horse's feet are very important. They should be balanced, with no underslung heel. Look for big, round feet, strong hoof walls and concave soles. Look at the foot from behind. Make sure the horse doesn't have sheared heels lacking symmetry and balance. Check to see that the bulb on one side is not higher than the bulb on the other side. The hairline should be the same distance from the ground on both sides.

Examine any abnormal condition. Can it be fixed or has it progressed to the point of indicating some permanent damage? For example, if I look at a 4- to 6-year-old with severe under-run heels, and the horse looks as if he's been the victim of poor shoeing, I don't consider buying him without a foot X-ray to determine if there have been any navicular changes.

Stifle. I first look at a horse's rear end from the side, so when I look at the stifle, I want to see that it sits well up under the horse. I want the femur to attach to the pelvis, far to the rear of the horse. Then I also want that femur bone to be long and reach well under that horse, to be angled out and away from the horse's body and forward, thus placing

the stifle joint well forward and angled away from the body. The angle of the stifle goes out and then back in toward the hock.

Just in front of the stifle is the horse's belly. As a horse is stopping, if the stifle hits the body, the horse's ability to stop deep and hard is inhibited. If his stifles are wide enough to pass beyond the back portion of his belly, the horse's ability to stop is almost unlimited. This power and freedom of movement are essential to a great performance horse, whether it be for reining, cutting or ranch work.

That's why it is very important, when looking at a horse from behind, that his stifles are the widest part of his rear end. For almost any rule, there are exceptions—but not in this case. A straight-stifled horse or a narrow-stifled horse cannot collect and, therefore, is mediocre at stopping.

Hock. When a horse has ideal conformation, you can draw a plumb line from the back of the horse's hip to the ground. With the horse standing so that his cannon is perpendicular to the ground, the hock and the

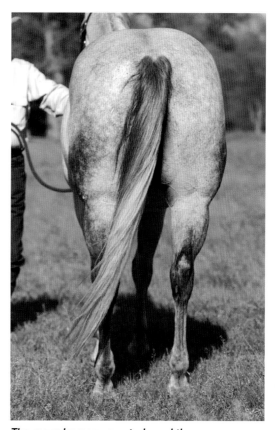

The more horses you study and the more ways in which you evaluate them, the better your eye becomes in recognizing quality conformation.
ROSS HECOX

back leg should fall at or slightly in front of that plumb line.

The post-legged horse, however, has a very straight hind leg. In assessing him with the same plumb line, you find that the hock and the back leg are substantially in front of the plumb line, but so straight up and down that maladies caused by concussion appear early in the horse's training. The horse with this type of conformation does not have as much freedom of movement as a correctly built horse and has more stress from concussion. This individual also has more problems with collection because of an inability to drive from behind, off the hindquarters.

On the other end of the spectrum, a sickle-hocked horse's hocks and back legs fall behind the plumb line with a great deal of angulation. His hocks are the opposite those of the post-legged horse. Because of the sickle-hocked horse's excessive angles, more stress is placed on the deep flexor tendons attached just below the hocks and down into the legs; this stress results in swelling. The sickle-hocked horse starts out like an exceptional stopper because his hock angles cause his feet to land well under his body. But that also puts undue stress on the entire suspension system of the back legs. With time, as a sickle-hocked horse continues to stop, stress to the tendons and ligaments in that area causes him to develop soreness, and his conformation predisposes the horse to curbs, or swelling in the hock, and other related problems.

Of course, a horse with normal conformation can develop a curb, too. For example, he might accidentally fall with all his weight on that specific area and hurt himself. In this case, the injury might bother him for a while but likely goes away and is never a problem later. But a horse that has a curb because of leg conformation usually has a chronic problem in spite of all the treatments.

For the sake of overall strength and continuity of the rear-end conformation, I like to see an adequately muscled gaskin that ties well into the hock and has sufficient muscling on the inside as well as the outside. These things contribute to overall strength in the hindquarters and are important factors in helping a horse use his hocks properly when backing with speed.

For the same reasons I want short cannons and long forearms on the horse's front end, I want low hocks behind because the

horse has short cannons. The shorter the cannon is behind, the lower the hock is to the ground, the more strength the horse has stopping, turning and rolling back, and the less stress there is to the hock in these maneuvers. When evaluating a horse, I make sure his hocks look low because of short cannons, not because there is too much bend in the hocks.

Look for a horse with a large, strong-looking hock. You should see bone and mass there that match the rest of the horse's body. If he's stout elsewhere, you don't want or expect the horse to have a fine little hock.

Lower hind leg. Below the point of the hock, I want to see a completely clean flat surface. Any roundness looks like a weak attachment to me. If I see a 4-year-old or older horse, and there is a little soft-tissue enlargement there, I don't worry about it. The horse probably works for a living.

In a 3-year-old or even a 2-year-old horse that's being ridden, I consider a windpuff, or puffiness in the fetlock joint, like a thorough-pin with swelling above the hock—a sign that the horse works. That isn't a problem unless a conformation flaw, such as a frail ankle, long sloping pastern or crooked ankle, causes the swelling. Any skeletal deviation a few degrees off from correct conformation is probably a warning sign.

Looking at the leg from behind, I think it's ideal that the bone from the stifle to the hock angles back and into the hock. The leg from hock to ankle should be perfectly straight and perfectly perpendicular to the ground. I can drop a plumb line from the hock to the ankle of a correct horse and the line mirrors the path of the leg.

The area from the ankle to the toe angles out slightly, similar to the way the stifle angles outward. A horse built this way has the strength to stop straight but wide. Stopping slightly wider behind is preferable to stopping narrow because of interference with the front feet. Every time the front end is stressed because the back end interferes, there is an increased likelihood of injury, stress, damage or mental strain on the horse because performing the maneuver hurts.

The ideal is a horse that stops wide with a great deal of strength. Then, once he is trained well, he is physically capable of holding himself straight all the way to the end of the stop. Another advantage to the horse stopping wide: If, at the end of the stop he needs to do

Quality conformation counts, but fitness makes a huge difference in a horse's appearance. Both of these well-built mares had successful careers. However, when these shots were taken, SR Glitter, the sorrel with white leg markings, was just in from the pasture to start under saddle, but the solid sorrel, Senorita Miss Cee, had been ridden for several months. The difference conditioning makes is obvious.

BRENDA PIEPER

Texas Kicker demonstrates the athleticism required of some performance horses; a poorly built horse simply cannot perform such a maneuver as well or for as long a period of time as a horse with sound conformation.

BRENDA PIEPER

a rollback, the wide base of support allows him to roll back over his hocks and leave the maneuver in one continuous motion.

The horse that stops with his feet very close together has a narrow base of support and must work hard to balance in the rollback. Think of a tennis player's "ready" stance—legs comfortably apart, knees bent, balanced and ready to move in either direction. Unlike that ready tennis player, the horse whose feet are close together behind first has to put himself into position to move before he begins any maneuver; his narrow stance is not an effective ready position.

There's a difference between stopping wide and "spreading" in the stop. Spreading is caused by cow-hocked conformation, or a horse leaning and pushing in the stop, or because the horse doesn't take a full stride and just jumps into the stop.

Belly. A reining horse needs to have a lot of strength over his loin, but the strength in the abdominal muscles is a real factor in determining which horse is a big stopper and which one is not.

Hollywood Gold, Jewels Leo Bar, and King bloodlines often have characteristic rounded bellies. Horses built that way usually are big stoppers. They are generally deep-bodied through the abdominal area just ahead of their stifles, and they have very strong abdominal muscles. Muscles exert strength by contracting and the contraction of belly muscles is what creates the classic, break-in-the-loins, deep stop.

Fish-bellied and slab-sided horses don't have strength in that abdominal area and are rarely able to achieve that kind of stop. These horses simply lack the power to hold themselves in the ground.

When considering conformation, remember that it's rare to find a great horse with poor conformation. It's even more unusual to find a great horse with poor conformation who stays sound for a long career.

In conclusion, I want to point out that a horse's hindquarters are the "engine" that propels the horse forward, balances his body, gives him the ability to turn 180 degrees or execute a flat, rapid spin. This is why, when considering a performance prospect, I am so particular about the horse's rear-end conformation specifically, as well as that correct conformation in general.

Section Three
Tools for Clear Communication

During his 2-year-old year, a horse is taught to move freely forward at all three gaits without any restriction. We spend a lot of time riding in the pasture, through woods and across streams—relaxing miles with no pressure on the young horse.

Seventy-five percent of our horses spend the entire 2-year-old year in a hackamore. With some horses, we do use a ring snaffle, but that depends on each horse. Some are more sensitive to their noses, others to their mouths. Personally, I think I can develop more confidence and keep a 2-year-old horse relaxed with less stress by using the hackamore.

As mentioned previously, other excellent trainers prefer to use snaffle bits from the very beginning and train some great horses. If doing that fits your style of riding, stay with a bit.

The important thing to remember is that these tools, and the other equipment we use in our training, are instruments that serve to better our conversations with our horses.

"I don't use more bit because I think I need more control; I make the change... when I'm ready for more refined communication... ."

5

Headgear

The headgear I use—bosals, bits, bridles and other equipment—has a critical effect on my ability to clearly communicate with horses, so it's important that I choose headgear carefully. Headgear selection is always an important consideration as a horse's training progresses.

Although many people start colts in a snaffle bit, I prefer starting a young horse in a halter, then go to the hackamore and then later change to a snaffle bit. When a horse responds well in the snaffle, the initial leverage-type bit I typically use is a short-shanked bit with a snaffle-type mouthpiece, followed by a long-shanked snaffle, usually a Billy Allen bit. After that, any one of an endless variety of bits might be selected for a particular horse.

In addition, I might use other equipment in conjunction with a bit to achieve specific things when I'm training a horse. But no matter if that item of equipment is a noseband or cavesson, a martingale of some sort, or draw reins, once I've accomplished what I set out to do, that added equipment goes back in the tack room and I resume riding the horse with only the bridle.

The Halter

The first day in the round pen, I start a colt in a halter and lead. I use an all-in-one, soft rope halter

and lead. I prefer the kind that ties below the horse's left ear as opposed to other types of halters because the rope halter with tie is far more adjustable.

The Hackamore

One of the most important tools used in my horse program is a hackamore. If a person is going to have only one hackamore-type noseband, the ¾-inch size is the one to buy.

If that's the case with you, try to find one made by a quality craftsman. You want the hackamore noseband to have a little weight to it. That's because a heavier-weight hackamore typically is of better quality than that found in a lighter-weight hackamore made in the same size.

It is very important that the hackamore noseband meets the horse's nose and jaw when your hand moves slowly to make contact; then the hackamore becomes a barrier when you increase the pull. If the hackamore is stiff, rather than supple, the response you get from the horse is one of resistance, rather than quiet obedience. So you also want a hackamore that feels soft and supple, and a fairly flexible hackamore usually is better made than the stiff one.

Make sure that the hackamore noseband has a rawhide core, rather than a core of cable. Cable cores are too stiff and a little too abrasive to the horse's

Headgear is one of the primary means through which you can speak the language of horsemanship.

The hackamore rein, the mecate, is long enough to make an adjustable loop rein, plus a "get-down" rope, shown hanging low on the horse's left shoulder.

ROSS HECOX

jaw. If your horse tends to have tender skin, use petroleum jelly on his jaw where the hackamore makes contact. Doing that helps prevent that jaw area from becoming sore. Remember: A horse responds softly to the hackamore until he gets sore, and then he stiffens with resistance.

A typical mecate, the rope rein used on the hackamore, is 22 feet long with one end wrapped around the hackamore heel knot. The remaining rope creates an adjustable loop rein with the excess length becoming a lead or "get-down" rope.

A horsehair mecate should be made of mane hair. Mane hair has a soft feel and is not as stiff as tail hair. Plus, mane hair maintains its consistency in the weather better than tail hair.

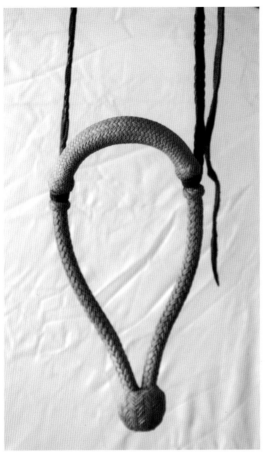

If you have only one hackamore, look for a quality ¾-inch noseband with a rawhide core, which has been made by a craftsman.
ROSS HECOX

Hackamore Maintenance

Since the hackamore represents a sizable investment, make sure to maintain your hackamore well. Old-timers used beef tallow— big hunks of natural beef fat in a bucket— all over the hackamore to keep it soft. Ray Holes' also has a rawhide cream that is a good option for most.

As for the mecate, clean it with Woolite®, then use fabric softener and hang the mecate to dry. Woolite removes sweat and the softener helps keep the horsehair easy to handle.

Hackamore Fit

The fit of the hackamore is adjusted by the number of wraps of the mecate on the heel knot of the noseband. The heel knot is important because its weight and the additional weight of the mecate wraps give an immediate drop when pressure on the reins is released. This instant release, obtained when the horse responds correctly, is the key to success in a hackamore.

A lot of people buy a hackamore that's too short, for example, 10 inches. This size gives little room for wraps around the heel knot, so you have no adjustment. You need a hackamore that's large enough to let you make the wraps and tie the mecate, yet still leave enough space for the horse's head to be comfortable.

Another common mistake for hackamore users is wrapping the mecate too tightly, which decreases the room allowed for the horse's nose. When that happens, the horse can't feel the release. The horse's skin gets numb because the tightness decreases circulation. When his nose gets numb, he loses his feel, and then becomes stiff and lethargic in the hackamore. Short, lightly taken wraps leave more room for comfort.

Even with a properly fitting hackamore, you want to adjust this headgear up and down the horse's nose as you use it to keep the horse from losing sensitivity. If you're riding a half-hour or 45 minutes, you might not have to move it, but when you ride longer periods of time, move the hackamore hourly about ¼- to ½-inch up or down the horse's head.

Just as with bridle and bit, the fit of the hackamore is critical to effectively communicating with your horse.
BRENDA PIEPER

Where the mecate loop rein comes out of the wraps—nearer the heel knot or more toward the noseband—helps determine the amount of lateral or vertical flexion you can engage while riding your horse.

ROSS HECOX

Getting Results

Where the mecate loop rein comes out of the wraps on the heel knot makes a difference in the feel of the hackamore, too. Reins that come out farther behind the wraps, nearer the heel knot, create more vertical flexion than reins that come out near the front of the wraps, closer to the noseband, which creates more side-to- side, or lateral, flexion.

Another factor that influences both the severity of the hackamore and how it works is the size of the nose button, which puts pressure on the horse's nose. The diameter of the nose button and the severity of the hackamore have a direct relationship—a smaller button means a more severe hackamore cue because the pressure is concentrated on a small spot. Conversely, the large-diameter nose button distributes pressure across a wider area.

Also, the shorter the nose button, the more leverage is created when you use the reins to pick up the heel knot. So the shorter the nose button, the more vertical flexion you have. The longer the nose button, the less leverage and the more lateral control you have.

Your reins should be adjusted so you can move your hands independently without one interfering with the other. There should be enough slack in the rein that you can pull one rein out to the side without the other rein being pulled across the horse's neck.

When using a hackamore, it is important to remember that it works on principles of a fulcrum and a lever. The balance point is where the hackamore hangs with no rein pressure. When the reins are picked up and the knot comes up, the noseband goes down and puts pressure on the nose. Generally, I ride most colts in the hackamore at least 45 days before putting a snaffle in the horses' mouths.

A larger hackamore nose button disperses pressure across a larger area, so is less severe than a button of smaller diameter, which concentrates pressure on a smaller area.

CHERYL CODY

The Ring Snaffle

When I begin riding a colt with a bit, I use a D-ring or an O-ring snaffle with a ½-inch-diameter mouthpiece. I prefer a D-ring to an O-ring because the feel of the D-ring is more like the hackamore than the feel of that O-ring snaffle is. The horse moves into the pull and away from the pressure coming from the flat side of the D-ring.

The colt is ready for the snaffle when he yields to a little pressure and allows me to give him direction. At this point he knows that a pick-up on the reins is a cue and he understands what is being asked of him. Only when he has learned and is comfortable with these principles is he ready for the unfamiliar pressure of a bit inside his mouth.

I like to let the snaffle hang ¼- to ½-half inch below the corners of the mouth to encourage the horse to pick up the bit with his tongue and carry it, rather than relying on that headstall to hold the bit in place. Too, in the beginning a bit can seem a little "gaggy" to a colt. After the horse gets better about picking up the bit, I can raise it until ultimately there's one wrinkle on each side of the horse's lips.

When using a snaffle, I prefer a browband headstall with a throatlatch. This keeps everything in place well and the bit hangs where I want it to be. I also like some form of curb strap under the chin, between the mouthpiece and where the reins attach to the D-ring. Later, when I change to a leverage bit, I like using a one-ear bridle with buckles on each side and a sliding earpiece so I can easily adjust the bridle to any size head.

I prefer ⅝- to ¾-inch harness-leather reins that are 7 to 8 feet long. Reins are a personal preference, but I want a thick rein, so the reins have some weight. As I lift the slack, the weight lets the horse know something's coming and gives him an opportunity to respond. Also, I get a more immediate release, due to the weight, when I drop my hand and release the horse.

Once a week or at least every two weeks, I go over all the bridles, headstalls and reins with leather conditioner and use olive oil on reins. I keep reins oiled so they have that lifelike feel, but I don't soak reins in oil because then they become mushy feeling. With a new pair of reins, I put them around a post and then pull them back and forth, like a shoeshine rag; that limbers up the stiff, new reins.

To encourage a horse to pick up and carry a snaffle bit, adjust it so that the bit hangs ¼ inch or slightly more below each corner of a horse's mouth.

DARRELL DODDS

Introducing Different Headgear

I normally like to introduce new things to a horse on Tuesday or Wednesday. After my horses are off on Sunday, I like to have a day or two for a refresher course in familiar equipment before I change anything.

Then, when I introduce a different bridle, I have three or four days to familiarize the colt with the new equipment before he has another day off. Whether I am changing from a hackamore to a snaffle, from the snaffle to a hackamore, or from either one of those to a short-shanked leverage bit with a snaffle mouthpiece, the transition should be smooth if I have done my work properly.

Of course, when using a new bit, I allow my young horse to acquire a feel for the new gear by riding him quietly for a day or so until I think he is ready to advance in his training. Rarely do I ever have to go back to his earlier equipment to reassure a young horse, but this option is always open.

The Pressure Areas in the Mouth

First, in the snaffle, a horse feels pressure most in the corners of his mouth. Then, as the horse becomes soft through the poll and learns how to carry the bit, the bit also exerts some bar pressure.
DARRELL DODDS

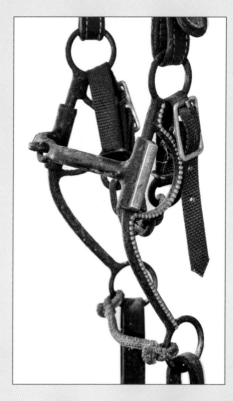

When the curb chain is introduced on a shanked bit with snaffle mouthpiece, pressure is applied to exterior points on the horse's jaw. That's because the mouthpiece's hinged center creates a scissor effect, so pressure is applied on the outside of the bars.
DARRELL DODDS

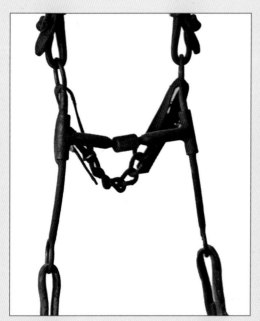

The Billy Allen mouthpiece with the roller in the center reduces the scissor action of the previously described bit, so creates a little more tongue pressure than that applied by a snaffle mouthpiece.
ROSS HECOX

Palate pressure is created with a high-port spade bit, which, when engaged, puts pressure on the roof of the horse's mouth.
DARRELL DODDS

Short-shanked bits are available with a variety of mouthpieces, and a horse often rides well in such a bit for many years.
ROSS HECOX

Short-Shanked Bit

The next standard piece of equipment I use is a short-shanked snaffle, as it's known, which actually is a short-shanked leverage bit with a snaffle mouthpiece. My favorite measures 2½ inches from the mouthpiece to the top of bit and 3½ inches from the mouthpiece to the center of the rings where the reins attach.

This short-shanked snaffle provides the first curb-chain pressure for the horse. I have some short-shanked snaffles with ½-inch mouthpieces and some with ⅜-inch mouthpieces. It is important to realize that the smaller mouthpiece creates a little more feel than the larger diameter mouthpiece.

A common mistake is adjusting the curb chain too tightly. It needs to be fitted so a horse can feel movement in his mouth and feel the chain rotate for a time before the curb tightens. I want the horse to respond to the bit, and the looser curb gives the horse a little more time to react. Also, if the curb is too tight, the horse never feels the release.

I prefer chain curbs with nylon buckles on each end. I find that the nylon holds up better than leather. Also, once the curb is adjusted, I don't want it to stretch, and sometimes the latigo leather straps do. I want single-link, rather than double-link chain, and one ½-inch wide.

This bit, commonly known as a short-shanked snaffle, is actually a leverage bit with a snaffle mouthpiece.
ROSS HECOX

Anytime you bridle your horse, make the experience a comfortable one; forcing the bit into a horse's mouth only makes him more apt to try and avoid being bitted the next time.
DARRELL DODDS]

Long-Shanked Bit

The next step is using a longer-shanked bit with snaffle mouthpiece. This bit measures 3 inches from the mouthpiece to the top of the rings where the bridle connects and 5 inches from the mouthpiece to the center of the rings where the reins connect. The longer shanks create more leverage than a shorter-shanked bit, more pressure with the same contact.

It's important to understand why I go to "more" bit with longer shanks. I don't use more bit because I think I need more control; I make the change when the bit I use gives excellent control and I'm ready to for more refined communication than I can have with the bit I've been using. The longer-shanked bit allows me to do that.

The Billy Allen bit comes next as a horse's training progresses. This bit works on sort of the same principle as the long-shanked bit described above, and creates something of the same feel. But because of the roller in the center of the mouthpiece, a Billy Allen bit is not as flexible as one with a snaffle mouthpiece. The Billy Allen mouthpiece with the roller introduces the horse to more

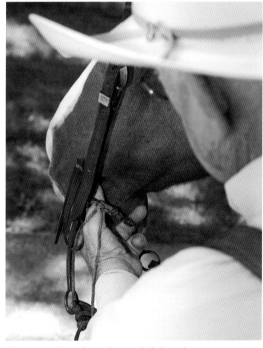

Use your thumb and your left hand to support and control the bit when you bridle your horse. Then he soon learns to accept this as part of his daily routine.
DARRELL DODDS

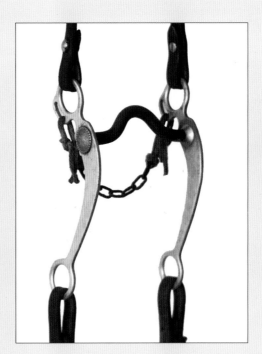

Not all fixed-cheek grazer-styled bits are the same, as the height of the port and the length of the shanks can vary, just as they can in many similarly styled bits.
ROSS HECOX

tongue pressure than he's had before, which is another area I can use to create sensitivity and softness.

A Variety of Choices

From the Billy Allen bit, I can choose from a relatively wide variety of bits. My choice, in many cases, depends on a horse's head, neck and mouth conformation. For example, a horse with a thick tongue needs a bit with a fair amount of port, because that horse needs some place for his tongue to go when leverage is applied. Also on a fat-tongued horse, a fair-sized port allows pressure on the bars.

I prefer bits made of black or sweet iron. I like the copper-inlaid bits because, like iron, copper seems to stimulate saliva. The least desirable metal is aluminum, which has a tendency to dry out the horse's mouth. Most horses seem to dislike the aluminum taste.

My bits are wiped off once a week with a rag dipped in corn oil because sweet iron can really rust.

The Cavesson

If I use a cavesson, or noseband, I don't adjust it too tightly. I want the horse to have room to open his mouth a little, but when he opens his mouth an excessive amount, the cavesson stops the movement. I prefer a lariat-rope cavesson that goes over the bridle.

Since the noseband on a rope cavesson isn't adjustable, I keep several sizes on hand.

When I first put a colt in a short-shanked bit, I don't use a cavesson. I let the horse open his mouth in the beginning because I find that, as he learns to respond to the suggestion of pressure, he usually stops gaping his mouth. If, however, a horse opens his mouth at the slightest touch, I use a noseband. Some horses seem to be a little mad about the noseband and fight and mess with it. If that's the case, it's better to forego using a cavesson.

Martingales and Draw Reins

I use a running martingale quite a bit. I like one that's easily adjusted because I use it on many horses, so must adjust it tighter or looser, depending on the horse. In the situation where I adjust the martingale shorter than normal, it's very important that I immediately adjust it back to the normal position as soon as I have accomplished what I want with the horse.

The preferred running martingale has a strap from the cinch that splits, and each end of the fork has a ring for a rein to go through. Another strap also goes around the horse's neck to support that fork and cinch strap.

The German martingale is just a regular set of reins that normally would attach to

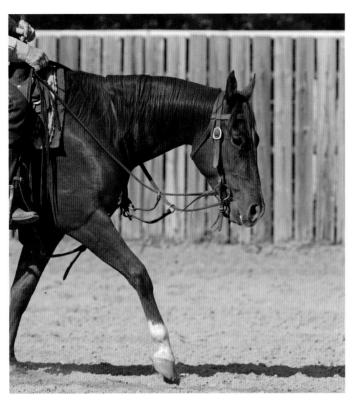

The key to using a running martingale or any such headgear is knowing how to properly adjust the equipment.
ROSS HECOX

Rings sewn into the bridle reins provide the means to adjust a German martingale.
DARRELL DODDS

A German martingale can work simply as a direct rein or much like draw reins, depending on how well-collected a horse travels in frame.
DARRELL DODDS

a snaffle bit, but now have rings sewn onto them. Nylon lines attach to a cinch strap and come through the bit rings to snap into the rings sewn onto the traditional pair of reins. The German martingale has the capability of working like draw reins when the horse's frame is out of position, but acts solely as a direct rein when the horse stays properly positioned.

I use draw reins only on rare occasions to soften a horse in the poll or from side to side. As with the running martingale, as soon as I accomplish what I want, I take off the draw reins and go back to normal equipment.

My draw rein is a long, continuous rein attached at the center of the cinch, the cinch dees or the breast-collar D-rings. From there, the long rein goes through the bit ring on one side of the bridle, over the horse's neck, through the bit ring on the other side of the bridle, and finally back to the cinch dee or breast-collar D-ring on the other side.

Draw reins offer an extreme amount of leverage for a horse that doesn't want to accept the barrier of the reins. When I use draw reins, I think of them as a medicine—not as everyday vitamins.

Remember: Draw reins are a prescription for a specific problem. With them, you can develop a horse that's behind the bridle and teach him to avoid the bridle just as easily as you can correct the problem of the horse not respecting the bridle.

With draw reins, just as with any martingale, the minute you accomplish what you want, go back to your horse's normal equipment.
DARRELL DODDS

Use draw-reins with caution; otherwise, you might well teach your horse to avoid the bridle and travel with his head behind the vertical.
DARRELL DODDS

6

Equipment

As with the headgear discussed in the previous chapter, other riding equipment needs to suit both horse and rider. The horse can't perform well when, for example, his saddle, pad or protective leg gear isn't comfortable due to poor fit or inadequate materials. Likewise, a rider can't focus on a successful training session when his saddle, for example, doesn't serve as an effective tool to help accomplish his horsemanship goals.

No matter what type of horse gear you might be purchasing, always keep in mind that two parties can benefit from the new equipment—you and your horse. Whenever a piece of new equipment catches your eye, take a minute to consider the item from the horse's perspective, too. When new gear can help make the horse's job easy that usually means your day's ride is pleasant, as well.

Saddle Fit

As mentioned previously, riding equipment needs to work for both the horse and the rider, and that's particularly true when it comes to the saddle. When a saddled horse can move his spine comfortably and freely under a saddle, he can pay attention to his rider's requests and respond well. Likewise, when the saddle is a comfortable fit for the rider, he can really focus on his horse and have a pleasant, successful riding session.

Horse fit. A saddle must fit the horse. Different horses have different back conformation, but I want my saddle to sit down as low as possible on the horse's back while still allowing plenty of clearance for the withers.

The width between the bars of the saddletree is important. Although a saddle that's fairly wide between the bars can fit a round-backed horse, when that saddle is used on a high-withered narrow horse, the saddle likely fits lower on the horse and can rub the top of the withers. Because I want a saddle that works on as many horses as possible, I want my saddle to be made with a moderate bar width. A horse with exceptionally high or narrow withers, or the horse with the broad, meaty withers might require a custom saddle to accommodate that type of extreme back conformation.

Rider fit. Besides fitting the horse, the saddle must fit the rider. A saddle should allow you to sit and ride as close to the horse's back as physically possible. You want to be able to sit comfortably in the middle of the saddle and have the ability to move forward if you need to do that, too.

There is a lot of variation in what people choose in saddles, based on each person's particular body build. For the person with short legs and a long torso, or someone who carries a lot of weight in the upper body, a more restrictive, close-fitting saddle is

Gear and equipment that fits your horse well also functions well for the horse—and ultimately for you and your riding program.

ROSS HECOX

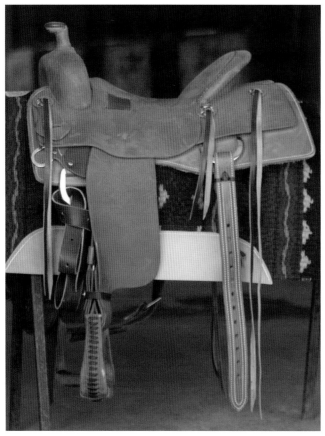

The saddle should be a comfortable fit not only for your horse, but also for you.

ROSS HECOX

good. This helps those people brace tightly with their higher centers of gravity. A long-legged person or one who doesn't carry a lot of upper body weight can get along in a less restrictive, loose-fitting seat, as that person's center of gravity is lower.

Saddle Parts

All the Dick Pieper saddles I have helped design are made on modified Bowman or Buster Welch trees. It took many years to perfect this saddle so it is as close to the ideal as any I've found throughout my career. This saddle fits a horse's back and puts the rider over the horse's center of gravity, and it remains one of the most popular saddles among reiners today. Below are some considerations about saddle features.

Saddle seat. You don't want a saddle that forces you to sit in one place due to the way the seat is constructed. You should be able to sit in the middle of the saddle and still be able to put your hand between the saddle cantle and your seat, so you aren't riding with your rear pressed back against the cantle.

That puts your feet too far forward for you to be able to use your legs effectively to control or cue your horse.

As far as seat size, a person who is long from hip to knee needs a larger saddle. That's because, when a person sits comfortably in the center of his saddle, it's very important that his heels naturally fall directly under the rider's spine. If one sits in a too-small or too-large saddle, the heels are either too far forward or too far back.

I like smooth seats. I see a lot of rough-out or quilted seats. I think a smooth seat lets me slide from one hipbone to another to clearly cue my horse. This factor is of major importance in changing leads, executing rollbacks and asking my horse to spin. A smooth seat lets me make small imperceptible movements more so than a rough-out seat.

Saddle front. In my all-around saddle, a very high front is a hindrance because I ride so much with two hands low in front. I make a bridge with my reins by crossing the reins and having a small amount of slack in between my hands. If a saddle has a high front, I can bump my hands or catch a rein on the saddle horn. With the lower front and a straight-up dally horn, I can still rope, even take my dallies, but at the same time have the luxury of no interference when I'm two-handed on a young horse.

Cinch. I use a high-quality 31-strand mohair cinch with a 4 ½-inch center width. This is comfortable for the horse and holds the saddle in place well without me having to tighten the latigo excessively. I think it's important to wash my cinches on a regular basis. For anyone riding more than one horse, I recommend a cinch for each horse, which makes it less likely to transfer any type fungus or skin irritation from horse to horse.

Billets. I prefer regular latigo leather billets. A lot of people use nylon and I have in the past. But when nylon becomes soaked with sweat and salt, the billet starts to deteriorate.

Stirrup leathers and fenders. I like a lot of flexibility in the stirrup leathers, from front to back. I like my stirrup leathers to swing freely from the horse's shoulder back to his rib cage with very little interference. This allows me to use my legs to cue the horse with both comfort and timing. I also like the saddle to be cut out underneath my thighs, which allows the maximum channels for my legs to have contact with the horse.

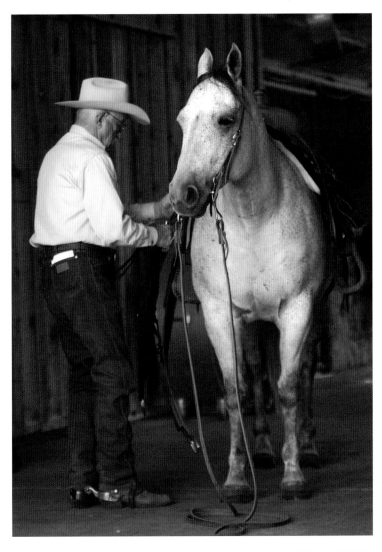

Keeping a cinch clean should be a part of any rider's routine maintenance program.
ROSS HECOX

A quality mohair cinch seems to hold a saddle in place well enough that the latigo doesn't have to be pulled extremely tight to stay in position.
ROSS HECOX

Maybe not the stirrup I would ride in every day, but it surely is nice for a show.
BRENDA PIEPER

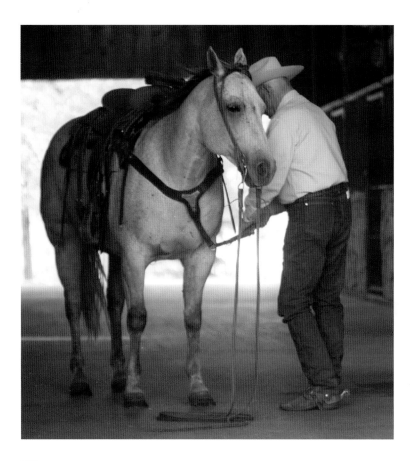

Stirrups. My favorite stirrup is a 2-inch-wide bell stirrup. This stirrup allows me to stand, press down, or rise up in the saddle to maintain balance. Riding on a 1-inch-wide stirrup is like trying to balance on a broom handle.

Saddle Pad

About the only saddle pad I use has a natural fleece lining and the Navajo wool cover on the outside. The pad is large enough to cover a lot of the horse's back and provides plenty of cushioning but not too much.

A good test of whether a pad provides enough protection is to squeeze it as hard as you can with your thumb and forefinger. If your thumb and finger are closer than about ¾ inch, then there is not enough padding to protect your horse. Too much padding can be just as bad as too little, causing the horse to get sore from having to be too tightly cinched.

Another advantage of the natural-fiber pad: It's absorbent, but dries quickly. This type pad is easy to clean with a gentle detergent for hand-washables and can then can hang on the fence to dry.

I want my pad to be a couple of inches larger than the saddle in front, in back and along the sides. I don't want the skirt of my saddle to overlap the outer edge of the pad anywhere so that my weight drives the edge of the pad into the horse's back. It's also important when saddling the horse to lift the front center of the pad into the saddle gullet so the pad doesn't bind the horse's withers and back when the cinch is tightened.

Breast Collar

If the saddle seems to slip, I use a breast collar that is V-shaped in front with a center strap to the cinch D-ring so that it doesn't ride up too high and interfere with the horse's breathing. Breast collars do not have to be pulled extremely tight the way a cinch can be. A breast collar only has to be buckled in the correct position, just to keep the saddle from sliding back. On many horses with good backs and withers, I do not use a breast collar unless I am roping and possibly dragging calves to the fire.

A well-designed breast collar that is properly positioned doesn't have to be really tight to do its job.
ROSS HECOX

Leg Gear

I like the wrap-support-type protective leg boots really well and use them daily when training horses. The boots offer both protection where a horse might strike himself and support for his suspensory structure, and I think that's ideal. Also, this type of boot is easy to maintain. I can take a pair off a horse, wash the boots, lay them in the sun and one hour later they are ready to use again.

For showing, I always use splint boots and I use rear boots on some horses when they are necessary. I prefer the splint boots with the double-sling suspensory straps because, of all the boots on the market, I believe these boots offer more tendon support than any other type. Because each boot has straps on each side that cross in front, this type of boot offers uniform support.

I do use bell or overreach boots a lot, but not for showing. As colts learn to turn around, some hit themselves in different places on the lower legs or pasterns. If I see that a horse has any tendency to hit himself, I always use bell boots. If I don't use the bell

A boot can provide both protection and suspensory support for a horse performing advanced maneuvers.
DARRELL DODDS

Bell boots can be of real benefit when a colt is learning to turn around or for any age horse that tends to strike himself.
DARRELL DODDS

boots and the horse hits himself much, he can develop a coronet-band abscess, which could turn into a quarter crack.

I use skid boots behind because I want to protect the horse's ankles. Skid boots also prevent him from feeling any discomfort there, which might cause him to not use his rear end correctly.

Spurs

As for spurs, in my tack room I have four or five pairs of spurs, each with a different rowel configuration. I use different spurs on different horses, depending on the sensitivity each horse has in his ribcage and behind the cinch. It's important to remember the spurs are used to cue a horse clearly and with a more subtle movement of the rider's heel. On very sensitive horses I use a cloverleaf-type rowel, probably the dullest rowel it's possible to have. On a horse that's not quite so "feely" or as highly sensitive as some horses might be, I use a six-point rowel that develops a little more feel without being too intense. On horses that tend to be a little dull, I use a 10-point rowel to help this horse feel the cue a little better than he might with, for example, the cloverleaf rowel.

It's important that your spurs don't fit snugly on the boots. The spurs should be loose so they freely move up and down the boot. Then, if the spur rides up, it falls back down and into place on its own.

In speaking of spurs, it's important to understand that spurs are tools for moving parts of a horse's body—not tools to make him go fast. If you use a spur to make a horse speed up, you also cause him to go fast when you try to move his hip or initiate a turn. These sure aren't times you want your horse thinking of increasing speed.

Remember: A spur is just an extension of your heel. As you progress to a sophisticated point in your training, you want to write with a pencil instead of a big fat crayon. That's always the role of the spur—to help the horse feel a cue and interpret it with substantially less leg pressure than you used in his early training.

A key point: If you have no need to cue your horse, keep your spurs out of his sides.
ROSS HECOX

Another key point: Spurs are tools used to move parts of a horse's body, not to make him run fast.
ROSS HECOX

With any equipment, try to get the best quality you can afford. A well-made piece of equipment from a superior manufacturer is really the cheapest to purchase in the long run because quality equipment lasts so much longer than poorly made gear.

The initial cost for protective leg gear might seem high, but it's worth it to help ensure that your horse doesn't suffer an unnecessary injury.
DARRELL DODDS

Section Four

Interaction Begins

In this section I begin to carefully engage an equine partner in conversation. It's often been said that the first thing a horse learns stays with him for the rest of his life. I wholeheartedly agree with this and this is why it is so vitally important that these moments of initial handling are done correctly. This is when it is determined if a horse ultimately becomes a willing partner or an unreliable and potentially dangerous mount.

*"... if you make sure that you take care
of every factor you can control, your odds
of success are greater...."*

7

Initial Handling

How a young horse is handled from the start has real bearing on how he interacts with people, as well as other horses, and how well he accepts training and performs as he matures. That's why we handle the babies we raise on the Pieper Ranch in very specific ways. We want them to have every opportunity to become solid citizens in the horse industry.

If you don't raise your own horses, but are looking for a young prospect, try to learn all you can about any young horse you're considering for purchase. Certainly it's good if you like a prospect's pedigree, conformation and attitude, but also ask exactly how he has been handled to this point. The more you know, the better you might be able to assess how the horse's early handling could affect the riding goals you hope to achieve.

Handling the Weanling

We wean our babies at five to six months, or earlier if feeding the foal is stressing the mare. Weaning and halter-breaking the babies are done in very stress-free manners.

We take each mare and baby through the stocks, as the horses already are accustomed to that and have been handled there previously for vaccinations and deworming. While the baby is beside the mother, one of us goes into the stocks with them and rubs and handles the baby until the baby is relaxed with a human touching all areas of his body. This approach is very similar to the technique of imprint training newborn foals, a way of handling newborns to prepare them for training later. In fact, this method in the stocks works even better if a foal has had the opportunity to be imprinted.

We then put the mare and baby in stalls in our breeding barn. These 12- by 24-foot stalls also are familiar to the horses, as that's where we put them when we bring mares in to breed or deworm. But each of those stalls has an extra gate that swings out to transform the area into two 12-foot square stalls. So now mare and baby are next to each other in these two 12-foot stalls, with a heavy wire panel gate that separates them, but still allows each full view of each other. The mom is relaxed and so is the baby. He can nuzzle his mom and nicker at her through the wire, but can't nurse. Of course, by this time the foal already is eating alfalfa and grain and has a great appetite.

We leave the mare and baby separated but next to each other for about three days until the baby is used to being in the stall by himself. During this period, we work on halter-breaking the foal, leading him around the stall, then around the breeding barn.

Pedigree, conformation and attitude are important when evaluating a prospect, but a foal's early handling also is a real consideration in how the horse might respond to training.
BRENDA PIEPER

These are the stocks we use to handle mares and accustom their foals to human contact in a stress-free manner.

DARRELL DODDS

Having the mare and foal adjacent one another gives each a certain amount of comfort and security as the baby learns more about people.

DARRELL DODDS

The lessons a horse first learns about pressure and its release during halter-breaking stay with that horse for a lifetime. When that initial experience is a good one, your horse program benefits for years to come.
DARRELL DODDS

Next, we take the mare to the pasture most distant from the baby. The two horses might nicker a day or two but they're not frantic. This is a very stress-free way to wean and how we handle weaning all our foals

After the foals have been in the barn alone for two or three days and they're not missing their moms at all, we let them all into a pasture as a group. We like to put an old barren nurse mare with the foals for security. She just acts as a sort of tour guide. If there's a thunderstorm, the babies run to her and she gets them through the process of starting to be little adult horses. We usually leave her with them until about December so she can show them the ropes. Shortly after that, usually in February or March, we separate the colts from the fillies to prevent the chance of an accidental pregnancy.

Halter-Breaking

However, while the mom is still close by and in full sight, I begin the training the baby, gently applying the give-and-take technique with the halter and the lead rope. This is the very first time I use the principal of applying pressure to receive a correct response in order to release the horse from the pressure.

It works this way: I put pressure on the lead rope by pulling the baby toward me. As soon as the colt takes one step toward me, I stop applying the pressure immediately to reward him. Giving to the pressure and taking a step toward me always results in a reward of the pressure stopping and the baby being rubbed and petted, especially on the forehead. This is a feel that he's learned when relaxing in the stocks.

Within a few minutes, it begins to be natural for the foal to step very lightly toward me to receive the reward. In the foal's mind, that reward is security. He now has had his first lesson in communication with a human. It's a lesson the foal easily can understand—and that communication results in something pleasurable.

However, I never overpower the foal physically. I want a mental acceptance, not a submission.

Throughout this early stage of training, the foal learns that closeness to the handler leads to a feeling of security. As soon as the handler

Pasture time gives my riding horse a nice break, the foals another experience with a human and me an opportunity to evaluate the herd.

DARRELL DODDS

steps away and gives a soft pull, the foal gives to the pull to gain security. Most smart babies take about five minutes of training on each side, right and left, especially if the foal is in the right mental state from the start.

The breeding barn facility is set up so it's easy to open the gate and take a brief walk with a baby around an already familiar area in the presence of the baby's buddies, and with minimal stress. In most cases, within 20 minutes I can lead the baby completely around the breeding barn. The mom usually is quiet because she can maintain eye contact with her baby.

Horse Colts

I geld a lot of our horses as soon as the colts are over the stress of weaning. When I look, for example, at the National Reining Horse Association record books, many of the solid campaigners who go on for years and years are geldings.

Each year, I pick out one or two of the fanciest colts—those that are bred well and out of proven producers—to leave as stallions. Although they have passed the first test,

these colts are on thin ice. When anyone sees the first indication that a colt wants to act less than perfectly, the colt is gelded. Remember: It takes a really good stallion to make a really nice gelding.

Life Outside

Once the foals are weaned and halter-broke, about all that's done with these youngsters is catching them for deworming, shots and hoof trims. They live outside until I bring them into the barn as long yearlings and start the breaking process, usually at about 20 months of age.

It's very important that these young horses get to live outside in groups and have other foals to interact with. The physical and mental growth that this environment offers is an advantage that stall-raised horses can't duplicate. The young horses growing up outside develop coordination, and going up and down hills and across creeks develops their strength and agility.

The interaction with other horses insures that the youngsters learn early on that there is a pecking order to the herd, so there's a mental benefit, too. Later, when a person comes along as the trainer, that's just another dominant player in the pecking order. The young horses also build their abilities to react to different situations and think under pressure as a result of running and playing together.

Potential Problems

For a stallion prospect, mental development is critical, so I don't leave stallion prospects by themselves. If they are, they can have some irreparable mental problems from the isolation. Once the fillies and colts have been separated, if I only have one or two colts, I put them in with a quiet old gelding—just to show them the ropes.

If you only have one weanling, he still needs companionship, even if you get him only a burro or another cheap baby horse as a buddy. In his formative time, a weanling needs company. The worst kind of horse to train is a backyard-pet horse. It is very difficult to predict that horse's actions because he has not developed normal equine responses.

That's the reason we don't hand-feed, brush, groom or teach little tricks to our babies. Instead, we allow them to be horses.

The goal in handling these horses during their childhoods is to give each baby a healthy psychological foundation.

For a performance horse, those first 20 formative months are incredibly important. If you buy a colt that is nutritionally deprived and has not had proper medical care, you're inviting failure. Likewise, if you buy a horse that has been isolated or made into a pet, you can't expect him to have a champion's attitude.

All these little factors—nutrition, health care, psychological conditioning—come together to form the raw material that helps determine a winner. If you neglect one area of development and your competitor in the arena doesn't, he can beat you later.

To win inside or outside the show pen, you're going to minimize your gamble by picking the right kind of horse, and then doing your homework to make sure that the horse has the best developmental foundation. Overall, your goal is to swing every part of the entire picture to your advantage. With a young horse, if you make sure that you take care of every factor you can control, your odds of success are greater than they would be otherwise.

Even though a foal experiences life outside with its dam, it's also important that after weaning a young horse can develop physically, mentally and socially in the pasture with the herd.

BRENDA PIEPER

"This initial handling also determines if a young horse ultimately can be a willing partner or could be considered unreliable and potentially dangerous."

8

The First Ride

You want to very carefully engage your equine partner in conversation. It has often been said that the first things a horse learns stay with him for the rest of his life.

I wholeheartedly agree with this. It is important that we begin our communication slowly and thoughtfully, quietly building trust and confidence with our equine partners.

The slower you work with your horse in the beginning, the quicker you can go later and the further your horse can progress. These moments of initially handling a young horse are vitally important and this early handling is where you lay the groundwork for a lifetime of riding. This initial handling also determines if a young horse ultimately can be a willing partner or could be considered unreliable and potentially dangerous.

Prep Work

The first day in the round pen, I start a colt in an all-in-one soft rope halter. I prefer the kind that ties below the horse's ear on the left side because it is more adjustable than a halter with a buckle adjustment.

When I first get on the colt into the round pen, I like to use the halter instead of a hackamore or bit because my objective in the first few rides is solely to get the colt accustomed to the weight of a rider on his back and to get the horse to move forward. The halter that I use in lieu of a conventional headstall feels familiar to the colt, as he's already been handled in it.

The worst thing I could do at this stage is use something harsh to pull him around because that only discourages a colt from going forward. The critical thing is that a rope halter is lightweight and doesn't give a colt any reason not to move freely ahead with good forward motion.

In an ideal program, a 2-year-old going to the round pen to be ridden for the first time is already pretty tame. He is fairly comfortable with people; he's been doctored, dewormed and trimmed, and is comfortable with being handled. Because he's been led, the colt knows what the halter is and how to yield to pressure from the halter on his nose.

I lead a colt to the round pen in a halter with an 8-foot lead. The saddle and pad are on the fence, but the first goal is to handle the horse and teach him to

Initial handling can affect how well or poorly a horse handles for a lifetime; take the time to make his early experiences good ones.

When helping a colt understand to go forward, how closely you step behind a horse's hip depends on the individual horse, but never put yourself in an unsafe position.

ROSS HECOX

free-longe. So I lead him close to the fence and then remove the halter and step away from the colt.

After I turn him loose, I step a little behind his hip so I can encourage him to go forward and move around the pen. My position behind and to the inside of the colt varies, based on his willingness to move forward around the pen. If he is reluctant to move, I might have to step behind him a little closer, but for safety's sake, I never get closer than six to eight feet behind the horse. An experienced horse person never puts himself in a position where he can be kicked. If the horse is still reluctant to step forward, I might use something like a longe whip—not to whip him—but as a visual aid to get him to move forward around pen.

Once a colt is moving and goes around the pen six or eight or ten times at a brisk trot, I back up to the center of the pen and say, "Whoa." The colt probably slowly comes down to a walk and then a stop, and looks at me. Then I step back a few steps to encourage

him to come toward me. If he does not come to me or his attention becomes distracted by him looking at other objects or outside the pen, I move behind the horse and make him go again. Then I try the whoa process again until I can stop and step back, and the colt moves toward me.

Once he steps toward me—with his attention on me—I walk to him slowly, pat him on the nose and rub him a little bit on the neck. Then I step to his other side and start him going in the other direction around the pen.

I repeat this same procedure until I can step back, take the pressure off the colt, let him stop and take a few steps in my direction—and he keeps his attention on me at all times. When I stop moving behind him, then back off and away from the horse, that's his cue that it's all right to slow down now and stop.

What actually is happening here: I am just beginning to show this colt that I am able to control him, control whether he moves or stops. It is to his benefit when he stops to

A young horse soon learns to stop when you step ahead of him to block his forward motion.
ROSS HECOX

take a few steps toward me because he has a chance to be patted and catch some air after being worked around the pen.

I want the colt to keep moving until I very obviously allow him to slow down or stop. This is the very first situation where I begin to show him that what I want him to do is easy and what I don't want him to do is difficult. This sets a theme for training going forward.

Typically, this session lasts long enough to get horse tired. He shows me he's feeling some fatigue though his demeanor; his neck comes down and he carries himself a little more efficiently. I almost see in his eye that he's gone from a fearful colt, feeling a little trapped, apprehensive and unsure of what to do, to one that has begun to develop a work-manlike mindset because he understands what I'm asking of him.

Again, I'm starting to exercise control over the colt and cause him to do what I want him to do. If the horse doesn't want to stop, I make him keep going until he does. I'm not much on jumping in front of a horse and

making him turn around. Instead, I simply restart him in the other direction after he stops and steps toward me and has been rewarded.

This process of becoming comfortable with going until he hears whoa, then stopping and being petted not only teaches a horse physically to free-longe around the pen, but also lets me begin to exert some control over him and his movements.

At this point, it's a judgment call as to whether I think the colt can handle it mentally to go on to the next step. When I can get a young horse to move around the pen, stop when I want, be relaxed and attentive but quiet, I'm at a good place and he's likely ready to advance. I'm looking to see that the horse is watching me, moving in a relaxed manner, responding quietly without panic, and acting like he enjoys the petting when he stops. For many colts that's a matter of 20-30 minutes. For others, the process might take longer but I always go at the colt's pace, not mine.

It's important to give a young horse time to accept the saddle pad or blanket as part of his normal routine.
ROSS HECOX

Rubbing a colt with a blanket helps him understand that he has nothing to fear.
ROSS HECOX

The Blanket

When the horse is comfortable in the round pen, moving around freely and stopping and coming to me, I begin to sack him out with a blanket, rubbing it all over his body and letting him get used to the feel of being touched in a way that is unfamiliar to him. I use a lightweight blanket that's easy to lift and rub it all over the horse until the young horse is comfortable with that.

When I introduce the blanket, I sometimes loop the lead one turn around the rail of round pen; I do not want the colt tied hard and fast so that he feels trapped. I hold the end of the lead with one hand and the blanket in my other hand, and gradually move near the horse to show him the blanket. I let him sniff the blanket and feel of it with his nose.

When he no longer is interested in that, I start touching his shoulder with the blanket, moving it against his skin in a circular or back-and-forth motion. I try to make this feel good to the horse, like a massage.

I watch to see that the colt is becoming relaxed about the blanket touching his left shoulder. When he's less wary, is not poised to move away and his muscles aren't tight anymore, I progress to his back and repeat the process. I touch, then rub his back with that blanket, all the time trying to make this a comfortable, enjoyable process for him.

When the colt is comfortable being touched on his back, I move the blanket to his hip, belly and so on. Then I do the entire process again on his other side—starting at his right shoulder. This process, time-wise, is all based on the colt relaxing before I move the blanket to the next part of his body.

During the process, it's important to remember to watch the colt carefully. If he's going to try to cow-kick me, he has to pick up his foot. If I see him pick up a hind foot, I move out of his kicking range and give him a chance to relax, as I go back and touch a part of his body where he's already comfortable with being touched. Then I move right back to the problem area and rub the horse again with the blanket.

Throughout the process, to get to this point, I just ask the colt to accept a little more and a little more—first dealing with the nearness of the blanket, then being touched by it. If the horse just refuses to settle down and accept me working with him, I make him exercise around the pen, then come back to work with the blanket again.

I continue this process until the colt is used to the feel of the blanket touching him all over and I can tell by his demeanor he's almost enjoying the rubbing. His eyes look soft and his muscles are no longer tense. Instead, he's relaxed with his head lower, maybe even has a back foot propped on its toe.

Then I rub the colt's shoulder and back some more, but this time I leave the blanket on the colt's back.

The Saddle

Next, I do the same things with the saddle that I have done with the blanket. As I approach the horse with the saddle, I let him smell and look at it. If he's really afraid at this point, I make him move around the pen some more before stopping him and going through the blanket process again. Usually, if a horse has become comfortable with the blanket, the saddle is not that frightening.

I set the saddle gently on the horse. Standing almost even with his front legs and facing forward, I reach slowly underneath the colt's body, catch the cinch and gently rub that cinch against his belly, just like I rubbed him with the blanket. When the colt accepts that, I slip the latigo through the cinch ring, double it and start to pull it. I pull only until the cinch just touches his belly. Then I rub the colt's belly and under the cinch against his belly, and rub his neck and pet him just a little bit.

I have everything set. I have the lead rope loose, where nothing can get tangled, and I pull the cinch in one motion and secure the tongue of the cinch buckle into a hole in that latigo. I don't tighten the cinch so much it's uncomfortable, but want the saddle to be secure enough not to frighten the colt by sliding underneath him as he moves. If this startles the colt, I just hold the lead rope. If the horse starts bucking, I just let him buck until he gets used to the saddle, and then catch him. Pretty soon he realizes that the

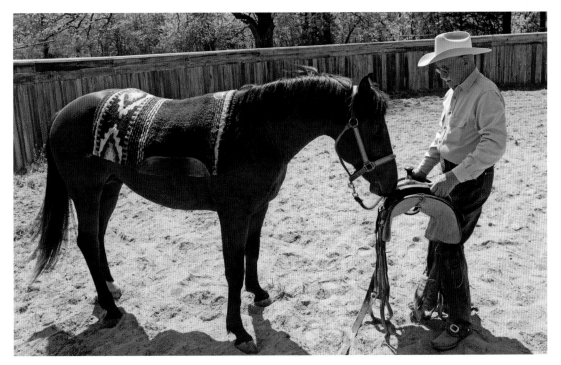

Letting a colt investigate the saddle reinforces the idea that it isn't harmful—and that you aren't either.
ROSS HECOX

Having a saddle slam onto his back can scare a colt, just like a predator's attack, so take care to let the saddle land gently on your horse.
ROSS HECOX

Reaching for the cinch is a prime time to use good judgment, just as it is when initially tightening the cinch.
ROSS HECOX

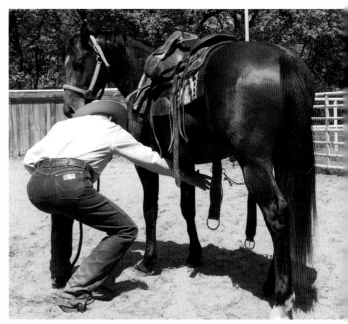

Once a colt is saddled, just ask the youngster to move around the pen; then give him time to become accustomed to the saddle on his back.
ROSS HECOX

When a horse focuses on you and steps in your direction, walk slowly toward him and rub him a little before resuming your work.

ROSS HECOX

saddle is nothing to be afraid of and I just catch the horse and go on with the process.

Now I hitch the lead around the saddle horn, tying the lead loosely. There is slack in the lead rope but the lead is out of way so that horse doesn't get tangled or step over the rope. Then I step behind the colt, just as I've done before, because I want the horse to move around the pen with the saddle on his back. If a horse doesn't want to untrack when he's saddled, I move a little more behind him than before and might even use the motion of the longe whip, if necessary, to get him moving, just like I already have done during the groundwork.

If the horse wants to buck, I let him. I just keep him moving around the pen until he relaxes with the saddle. This saddle creates a different feel for him and it takes a few moments, usually, for him to get past the new sensation. As the horse moves around with this foreign object on his back, he might kick at it to see if he can make it go away, or try to touch or shake the fender with his mouth. And a colt might simply go around the pen and never seem to be bothered by the saddle. Every horse is different.

I watch the horse for signs that he's accepted this saddle. I want to see that he moves comfortably around the pen. His eyes should be soft again and his gait relaxed. The colt must put his attention back on me. When

A colt's familiarity with the halter and lead provides him some basis for understanding when that same headgear is used for the first few rides.

ROSS HECOX

he is comfortable with the saddle, I let him stop and come to me; then I untie the lead and pet him gently.

The First Ride

Inasmuch as this first saddling and the first ride are stressful, I don't want to worry the colt more than he is already by putting some foreign object in his mouth. He's never before

First put weight in the stirrup for only a few seconds and step down; then repeat the process again and again. This is the point when you seem most like a predator to the horse.

ROSS HECOX

necessarily become second nature on the other side until the action actually has been done on that second side. A horse does not relate that something that is okay on the left side is going to be okay on his right.

If the horse is nervous, I don't proceed any further until he's relaxed. Some horses might just stand there, some might jump away, some might step way. When a colt jumps or moves, I step down and do things again and again until a colt stands quietly as I put my foot in the stirrup, step up, then down and on both sides. I put a lot of emphasis on looking at that colt's eyes and ears to determine if he is relaxed and quiet or if he is still nervous and apprehensive.

When the young horse is comfortable with me putting weight in the stirrup, I again hold the lead in my left hand, put my right hand on the horn, and step into the stirrup—but this time I swing my leg over him. I pause there in the saddle seat for a second, then just step off and do the same thing again and again until that process feels comfortable to the horse. If he wants to bolt, I just step back on ground. If he bucks, I do the same thing— step back on ground. If he starts to leave in any way, I just step down.

After I've gotten on and off the colt several times, I get on, put my right foot in the stirrup and sit down. Then I ask the horse to move by smooching to him and bump-bump-bumping with my legs. If he doesn't move, I bump a little harder; when he does take a step, I stop bumping the colt. When he takes a step or walks forward, that's what I want.

Throughout the process, I watch the colt's eyes and ears to read his reaction. If a colt is going to do anything, this is the point when he usually does it. If he takes off, I just have to ride through it. At this time, I think the worst thing I can do is try to restrain him. The horse needs to know that the rider and saddle are there and that there's no way he can outrun them; so if he wants to run, I let him until he chooses to stop.

If the colt wants to buck, I pick up on the lead rope and try to talk him out of that— maybe by bringing his head around to the side with the lead rope. I don't get really aggressive, just try to communicate to him, "Hey, you don't want to do that."

It's usually pretty easy to talk a colt out of bucking if you just pick up lead rope and pull him around and let him relax. If he really wants to keep bucking, which is rare, you just have to ride it.

felt pressure in that area, so the first time I ride him, I really like to use the same soft rope halter and lead that I've been using throughout the round-pen and sacking-out processes.

The first step in making the initial ride on a young horse is to put a foot in the stirrup, step up, stand in the stirrup a couple of seconds, then go back to the ground. I hold the lead in my left hand, usually put my right hand on the horn, and step up and into the stirrup. I get on the young horse on the left side first, several times, and then repeat the process on the right side.

I do this because a horse does not relate that what happens on his left can happen on the right. His brain has two sides; what is second nature on one side does not

If you're not confident that you can ride a colt through the bucking, or if you can't stay on him and aren't confident that you can get back on the horse and ride the second time, you need to send your horse to someone who can. This is not a place for a rider with novice skills. A rider's fears can create a negative situation with a colt and, worse, there is the chance for the unskilled rider to be injured.

Depending on your skill level, the safest thing to do, when a colt bucks, is to step off the horse and exercise the horse until he is more accepting of a rider in the saddle. It's important to realize that starting a colt with his first ride is not for everyone. If your skill level makes you feel apprehensive, at the very least you are going to transmit that to the colt and make him the same way.

A colt's first ride is no place for a novice or any rider lacking the confidence to deal with whatever might happen when the horse initially moves forward with a person on his back.
ROSS HECOX

Use the lead to guide the colt and also take a careful and quiet approach to moving the lead from one side to the other.
ROSS HECOX

The colt eventually does relax enough to advance to the next stage of training. He starts walking around the round pen in a relaxed manner, not quite sure of what's going on, but willing to accept this process of having a rider on his back.

From this point forward, whatever I do depends on what the horse does. If he stops, I shift my weight slightly forward and use the halter lead to guide him around to go in that other direction. To get the lead from one side to the other, I carefully and quietly swing it over the horse's head. Most colts are not frightened by this, as they have become accustomed to the lead moving around. However, when I swing the lead, I make sure there's a lot of slack in the rope so it doesn't graze the colt's ears, and I swing the rope very slowly so it doesn't startle him.

I try to walk a colt both ways around pen and maybe urge him to trot both ways. Then I get off the horse, loosen the cinch, lead him around for a minute or two, unsaddle and put him away.

At this time, I don't really give the horse direction; I just get him used to going forward. I don't make any attempt to give the horse direction other than occasionally to pull him around with the lead. He's in a 60-foot round pen; where can he go?

No matter what the horse does while I'm on him, I don't try to stop him. He eventually stops after we've gone around the pen a couple of times. I don't get on or off unless the horse is standing still. When he does stand still and I'm finished for the day, I get off the horse. In most cases he's tired and likely lets me carefully swing my leg over his back and step down.

I repeat the entire procedure the next day, beginning with sacking him out until he pays no attention to it. Then I saddle and get on him and let him move freely at whatever pace he sets. I just move that lead quietly from one side to the other to pull him around so he can walk both ways around the pen.

Usually after three to five rides in the round pen, a colt gets to the point I can quietly saddle him, get on and ride him. Only when he is comfortable with that am I ready to start steering the horse. At this time I don't try to control his gait or speed; we just ride at his speed until the horse realizes speed is not required. Because I'm still using a halter, a colt can run or buck. But he quickly finds that when he does, he gets tired, so he breaks to a trot, then a walk, then stands still.

All I want to do is stay on the colt and not do anything to further excite or stress him. He then finds that he's the one causing the stress, getting in a hurry. I really don't want to do anything to try to make him slow down.

Transition to the Hackamore

I know when I'm ready to transition a colt to the hackamore. That's when the young horse stands still for me to get on and off, and I can quietly nudge him with my legs and he walks around the round pen. I also carefully can ease the lead from one side of his head to the other and guide him in one direction around the pen or the other.

I don't keep a colt in the halter and lead more than a couple days. Three or four days' time is at the longer end of the scale. I just wait until he's relaxed and comfortable with what we've been doing.

Then he's ready for what I call a soft, non-confrontational hackamore. I use one with a big, fat rope noseband and jute reins about 1½ to 2 inches wide.

With the hackamore I teach the horse to respond to pressure on his nose, using a direct rein to the left or the right. For example, as he

This soft, braided rope hackamore is mild, so this headgear doesn't abruptly bite a colt's head and scare him if he makes an incorrect response.
ROSS HECOX

The transition to the hackamore provides the opportunity to teach a horse to stand quietly for mounting, as well as allowing more control.

ROSS HECOX

walks forward, when I ask the horse to move to the left, I lift the slack out of the left rein, put a little pressure on it and then put my left elbow back to my left ribcage—and I just hold. He might pull hard against the rein or put his head up and down, but I just hold the rein steady against my ribcage. The holding I do becomes like an immovable object.

The reaction I want from the horse is for him to realize that he's pulling against himself. I hold and hold until he relaxes his neck and becomes soft without pulling against my hand. As soon as he relaxes and feels the slightest bit soft, I move my rein and elbow forward and give him a great big release.

Then I repeat the same thing on the same side—pick up my hand, make contact and then put my elbow against my ribcage. I hold until he relaxes his neck and feels soft. As soon as colt figures out he's pushing or pulling against himself, things get easy in a hurry, as long as I repeat this process again and

again. A colt gets to where I can't get to his nose because he learns that if he gives to the pressure, the pressure goes away.

It's also important for the horse to understand that I want forward motion as he gives his nose from side to side and we do this first at a walk. When he's accomplished that a walk, I ask him to learn to give his head in the same way at a trot.

I work on bending the colt around in one direction for a while. Once he has mastered that, I give him a short break. Then I ask him to bend in the other direction by picking up the direct rein on the other side and, again, maintaining pressure until the colt gives his head in that direction.

Once the horse has started to bend his head from side to side, I then can ask him to back by making contact with his nose. Now I hold pressure on him until he steps back one step, then release him. All I do is put him in a pressure situation so when he feels the

Before working on the stop, first teach a colt to back by holding pressure on his nose until he takes just one step back ...
ROSS HECOX

... and then immediately release the pressure. In other words, let the colt learn to release himself from the pressure by stepping backward.
ROSS HECOX

pressure, he learns how to release himself from it by stepping back. When he does, I pet the colt and rub his neck.

For a period of the next few days, I work with the horse until I can get one step back consistently and am sure the horse knows how to respond to that pressure. Then I ask for two steps back before he gets a release, and then three steps and so on until he continues backing until I give the release.

Stop and Go

As soon as I can get on a young horse with a minimum of free-longeing, I ask him to trot. I give him the grown-up cues—slight squeezes with the calves of my legs. If necessary, I then bump his sides with my heels or the sides of my feet to get the point across to him in baby talk. That always is the process—the horse first gets the grown-up cue, and then if he doesn't respond, I reinforce the cue. The idea is that eventually the horse learns to react to the first cue and doesn't need the additional reinforcement.

Even during the first rides, the horse learns that leg pressure means to move and go forward. At this point, I don't wear spurs because I don't want to scare the young horse. Throughout training, I give him the light adult cue first, and then if there is no response, I follow that initial cue with simple, more forceful ones by bump-bump-bumping his sides. Now, I'm to the point that I have a little control. The horse is starting to respond to pressure from side to side and also is learning to go forward.

Now it's time to teach a stop. In my program, backing lays the groundwork for the stop. Pressure on the colt's nose means for him to move backward. It's logical that if he's moving forward, pressure on his nose can make him stop since he must stop before he can take a step back.

So next, I ask the colt to stop by lifting the slack from the reins, making light contact with the horse's nose. As soon as he stops, I release the pressure on his nose. If he doesn't stop right away, he does eventually. I keep the pressure on his nose and again hold. I might go around the pen three times while the colt keeps going, but he stops eventually. When he does, I give him the release.

Outside Riding

My goal always is to get a horse out of the round pen. I leave the small round pen pretty soon if a colt is really nice and making progress. I have a 60-foot round pen and a 150-foot round pen, which are connected by an alley. When I've had two or three rides on this colt and he's going around, knows how to stop to get a release and knows how to turn, I open the gate from the small round pen and go into the big round pen.

Once a colt has relaxed in the big pen, usually after four or five rides there, I open the gate and take him outside. If he's nervous, I keep him in the pen until he relaxes. There's not a set time frame for a colt to be ready to go outside; normally it takes more than two rides, but usually less than two weeks. I'd say the average is about a week in

What Else Should He Know?

While a colt is getting an education under saddle, he also learns how to be a well-groomed gentleman. He's already had his feet trimmed, and he now should be learning to stand quietly while being brushed and clipped.

When clipping a horse, one thing detrimental to future quietness during this task is using a twitch immediately when first clipping a young horse's bridle path or ears. Although a twitch can make a young horse stand still while being clipped initially, the twitch also enforces the idea that clipping hurts.

Instead, I introduce the clippers in same place that I ground-tie and saddle a colt, so it's a familiar area. I start the clippers, aware that the noise might startle him. When he accepts the sound, I move around him with the clippers running until the colt relaxes, finally bringing the clippers closer to his nose. The horse might pull back but I stay persistent and continue bringing the clippers near him. If he runs backward, I lead him back to his original spot. I just want the colt to become comfortable with the sound of the clippers.

If—on the second day—I'm to the point that I can clip three nose hairs, that is fine. I just want the horse to become less fearful each day until he's not afraid of clippers at all. But if I make a big deal out of it—forcing the horse by twitching him—then clipping becomes a bad experience and he hates being clipped or next three or four years.

Riding outside the pen allows a young horse to experience so many things, which builds the horse's confidence, as well as the rider's confidence in the horse.

ROSS HECOX

the round pen before I start riding a horse outside.

At that point, I ride through the woods and across creeks. I love to ride colts in the pasture because I can expose them to so many things—and that builds confidence. And at this point I don't ask this young horse to respond with a lot of finesse. The main goal is to get him to move forward and be confident with that forward momentum.

A complete willingness to go forward and to think forward is the first step to achieving collection with a horse. It's a mistake to try and get a horse to walk little circles and do lateral things at this stage. He first has to understand how to willingly and freely move forward to be ready for the basics.

My pulling on the horse or putting pressure on the hackamore at this point is just to herd the young horse along in the right direction. I want to put a lot of miles on him with no pressure whatsoever. This stage of riding a young horse lasts from a month to six weeks. Then the colt is ready to learn the basics.

Ground-Tying a Horse

Having a horse stand without being tied, or ground-tying, is something I teach all the horses at the ranch. When a colt is to a stage that he's fairly easy to saddle and ride is when training for ground-tying starts.

I do it in the barn hallway, right in front of the tack room. I lead a horse to that particular place, drop the lead to the ground and start to brush him. If he moves a foot, I simply take that lead, say, "Whoa," and move him back to that spot where he was. This isn't a punishment—just a correction. As soon as his feet are right back where they were, I drop the lead to the ground again and brush him again.

As soon as the horse steps forward, turns his head to look at something, or moves a foot, I push or pull him back into the original spot with the lead rope and again say whoa. Each time he moves, he gets that little reprimand that moves him back to the same spot. It's a matter of repetition—not overdoing the correction—but definitely not overlooking it anytime the horse moves.

I can see when the concept is starting to make sense and that the horse understands he's to stand quietly in same spot. I know he understands because he doesn't move, his ears are relaxed, there's a mellow look to the eyes, his head is level—he's a relaxed, quiet horse. And he understands because he doesn't move any more.

The horse doesn't have to stand like a statue with all four feet rooted, but can look around slightly. This can vary with different colts but, on average, one can be tuned into ground-tying within a week. The first morning, the training might take 20 to 25 minutes, then gradually less time, and in a week he should be pretty sure that he should stand there. Then, I drop the lead and walk into the tack room. That's only 10 feet away but I watch the horse all the time. If he moves, I go and put him back into his spot.

One young horse with a short attention span might not get the idea of ground-tying as quickly as another horse. As when doing anything with horses, repetition is a fact, and I keep on trying until the horse grasps the concept. Fillies might be a little easier to teach to ground-tie than colts, who might be a little more distracted. I don't think there's a big difference—just the matter of making sure a young horse knows it's important to stand quietly.

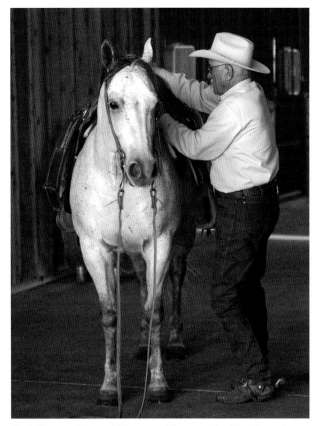

Saddling and unsaddling provide opportunities to make ground-tying a routine part of daily life.
ROSS HECOX

I keep working on ground-tying a horse until I can walk in and out of the tack room, and the horse stands there. I go in and get the blanket, then go back for the saddle, then get the hackamore—and he should stand there. Whenever a horse moves or loses focus, I go put him back into his spot. I do this every single day and in the same way.

When the young horse gets to the point he understands to stand there quietly, and gets pretty good at this, I take him to the round pen, and when I get off and loosen the cinch, I drop the reins. I go through the same process of correcting him in the pen, taking him back to the same spot, until he understands he's not supposed to move even though I have dropped his reins.

At some point I leave him ground-tied in the round pen while I ride another horse around him. If the ground-tied colt picks up his feet or starts too move, I get off my riding horse and correct the ground-tied horse, then go back to doing the same thing again. After a month or two, I can ground-tie a horse out there and ride another horse—and the ground-tied horse doesn't move.

Section Five
The Foundation

The first goals for the prospect to master are three responses.

1. The horse should be very flexible from side to side, soft and giving. When I pick up on one rein, even a slack rein, he should start to give his nose without me having to exert any pressure.

2. When I take up slack in both reins, the horse should step forward into the bridle. I want him soft in the poll so I can squeeze him forward with both of my legs.

3. The horse also should move away from pressure from either one of my legs. My right leg moves his hip to the left; my left leg moves his hip to the right.

That's all I require of a prospect. If he knows these things, he can back, walk, trot and lope, and he has the foundation for every maneuver I teach him as a reining horse.

Perfecting these basics to the point that the horse responds to the bare suggestion of a cue is the goal. Finally mastering these things signals that the horse is ready to move into actual reining training.

> *"The beginning of number one is lateral movement with the head. The completion of number one is a lateral move with the foot."*

9

Basic Number One: Giving to Pressure from Side to Side

When a colt is to the point that he's quiet and has accepted carrying the saddle and the rider's weight, he's ready to learn the basics. The horse and I have met; we've had contact. Now it's time to go to work and create the base for our language so we can increase our communication.

No matter what the intended use of the horse, the very first thing I teach him is what I call basic number one. This one response is literally the foundation building block of this language the horse and I are creating. How well the horse masters this first basic usually predicts how adept at communication the young horse can become.

The importance of this basic is evident in the way I refer to it at any time in the training process: "You need more number one," or "You've got to go back to number one."

If your number one is not working, you're losing communication, your horse is confused, or something is wrong.

The First Basic

Number one is the horse giving from side to side. When pressure is applied to the rein, the horse should give his nose, his poll, his neck, and then his shoulders in that direction. He should step willingly in the direction of pressure.

That's the physical description, but the psychological effect of number one is just as strong. Basic number one must be so firmly established in this horse that he responds without thinking. That response must become a reflex because that reflex of acquiescing—not resisting—is an indication of a mental acceptance that is large.

No matter how eager you are to begin building the foundation for advanced maneuvers, first be sure your young horse is really comfortable with the saddle and you on his back.

ROSS HECOX

In other words, when the rider gets on the horse's back, there is nothing in the world more important to this horse than listening to what the rider has to say. No matter what the horse's priority or interest at any time, when the horse feels the rider pick up on the reins, the horse should respond. His communication with the rider takes priority over any other agenda the horse might be entertaining.

The Initial Reality

When you first get on a colt and make contact by putting pressure on the rein, if he's like most colts, he stiffens his neck in resistance, pulling away from the pressure. The colt isn't very soft in hand, or very light. That's because his defense mechanisms have kicked in. The first response—flight—is restricted, so the colt tenses. Stiffness, resistance, resentment are uppermost in his mind. That's not a learning mode.

Part of what mastering basic number one must do is show the colt that pressure from the rider is not something the horse should brace against to protect himself from possible pain. Instead, pressure from the rider means that the horse is being asked to do something.

A young horse's typical reaction is to brace against the pressure, which gives you an opportunity to teach the release and give him a reason to respond differently to that pressure.

ROSS HECOX

When he does whatever that something is, he is rewarded.

That's why, when working with a young horse on basic number one, it's very important that I carefully monitor my actions to make sure that I communicate exactly what I want—and don't reinforce the horse's natural tendency to avoid the pressure. That's why I take things one step at a time.

The First Lesson

In the beginning on a colt, I walk a young horse in a lot of circles. I have the horse in a hackamore or in a D-ring snaffle. I lift the slack on one side, and take the horse's nose; in other words, I put pressure on his nose. In these initials sessions, when I pick up the rein, I keep my hand low, but out to the side—about a foot to foot and a half out—and level with my hip. If there is any resistance to the pressure, I hold, maintaining the pressure until the horse stops resisting. Then I give back to the horse, releasing the pressure. Then I repeat this process with the horse—many, many times.

When you do this, don't bend your wrist to pull the horse's head; the movement should be in your shoulder joint, with just a slight giving in your already bent elbow. Your thumb should be up, and the palm of that hand facing in and downward. Look at the line that the rein and your arm make. There should be a straight line from the bit to your wrist to your elbow.

As you pull, your weight should shift slightly to your outside hip and you then have more weight in your outside stirrup. Sitting on your outside hip puts more of your weight to your outside leg and stirrup. By sitting this way your outside leg is closer to your horse's body than your inside leg, which is out and away from the horse's side to open the door for him to go in that direction. You also are sitting in a position where you can hold on to the horse pretty well if he really resists you or really leans on that hackamore rein.

Now if I was in that situation and trying to talk to a horse with only my wrist, he could just take his head away from me and go on his way; so it's obvious that body position has become very important. Although at this point my body position is no different than any other rider position to this green horse, my position now is consistent with what my body position should be later when I begin to ask for a spin or a rollback. As always, my

It's so important to hold and maintain that pressure, and simply give the horse time to figure out how he can get that release.
ROSS HECOX

goal is continuity; I use this body position from the beginning so that the colt associates my position with giving and bending.

To Reach an Understanding

When you're trying to get a colt to understand softness and the release of pressure, sitting in the same position every time helps him understand what you want him to do. While he's working to understand, you don't want to distract him by changing position and being inconsistent. His response can be much better if all he has to concentrate on is your cue on the rein.

When you ask the horse to bend and give, never make a quick pull and, especially, don't jerk or bump the horse. Instead, take your hand out to the side, lifting the slack and softly making contact with the horse. Then increase the pull to bring the nose to the point you want it in the direction you're asking him to go. Once you move the nose to that tipped position, you hold steady—neither increasing nor decreasing pressure—until the horse softens and releases himself by giving. Then you immediately release the pressure.

Repeat the process. Remember not to jerk, but to pick up smoothly on the rein and increase the pressure to that desired point, then hold steady until you get the desired response. As soon as the horse softens, reward him by releasing the pressure.

At first, you reward the horse for even the slightest move in the correct direction. Remember: Your goal at this point is to show him that there is a "right" answer to the question you are asking.

"Can you give me your head to the left?" (The rein is picked up.)

"This much?" (The horse shifts his head to the left.)

"Perfect." (You release the pressure).

Now, in the beginning, the conversation might not go exactly that smoothly. Instead, the scenario might be more like this:

"Can you give me your head to the left?" (The rein is picked up.)

"Stop that! Let me go!" (The horse pulls away from your hand.)

"Ouch, that hurts." (The horse bumps against the bit being held steadily in the same position.)

Even though a horse might show some signs of softening to the pressure, it's critical to maintain your hand, arm and body position consistently until the horse truly gives to the pressure.
ROSS HECOX

105

"I'm going to pull until you let loose and give to me." (The horse continues to resist the steady pressure.)

"I'm going to turn my head to the left." (The horse moves his head to left.)

"Thanks." (You release the pressure.)

It's a little hard to understand, at first, but the essence is that I am not pulling on the horse after I establish that point for pressure. If he leans on my hand, I hold him, but I don't bring my hand back any farther than that point I have established. I am letting him pull against me. When he quits pulling on me is when I give him the release. There is certainly pressure involved. If he pulls really hard on me, I might be using all my strength to hold the bridle rein, but I don't pull back on him. Altogether, my arm, my hand and my elbow become a stationary object and this horse is pulling on it. When he stops resisting the pressure, I am going to release him.

It's really important to have steady hands. If you hold and hold, and have been pulling hard, when he releases, you really pull way back much harder than before. Then you have reinforced that this process is a tug-of-war. When the horse gives the correct response, you must reward him immediately in order to teach him that softening to pressure gets him a release. Eventually, as the colt understands more and more what you are asking, you are able to ask more of him, but the amount of pressure needed can decrease.

The Big Release

Another really important thing about this process of teaching a horse basic number one: When you give the horse a release, you must give him a big release. A lot of people, when a colt gives a little bit, give back only a little bit; the person might move his hand a half-inch. It's easier for that colt to understand if you give him a big release. When he gets soft and releases to that pressure, drop that slack a foot! Let him know that he gets a complete release when you turn him loose.

When the horse responds and gives to pressure, always be quick with your release and make it a big one. Then he understands— and that's communication.

ROSS HECOX

Simultaneous learning is part of developing a broke, responsive horse. It's okay, for example, to let a young horse extend his trot...
ROSS HECOX

... and begin to lay the groundwork for rating a horse by asking him to slow to a jog.
ROSS HECOX

leg first although the horse doesn't know that means to lope at this point. I follow that by "smooching" him up into the gait I want. The important thing: Even though the horse at first doesn't respond to the "grown-up" cue, I cue him with it each time. Then later it is natural for him to respond to that cue, rather than wait for the reinforcement to respond.

111

Q&A: Basic Number One

Do you teach a horse to go straight at this point?

Not necessarily. I think a better term at this point would be "forward." The idea is that the horse gives his nose and he moves in that direction while moving forward in an obedient responsive manner.

If a colt gives you his nose, but isn't going anywhere, do you go ahead and use your legs a little bit?

If he gives me his nose and is just being limber-necked and not going anywhere, I increase the pressure on the rein and make him move. I might take him real deep, in other words, increase my rein pressure even more to make him go somewhere and maybe encourage him just a little with the calves of my legs. But I want to stay away from using my legs during this stage as much as I can because I want the horse to learn to respond primarily to the bridle rein. If he doesn't want to give, I just increase the rein pressure pulling his head to the side more until he does move. If I pull the rein around far enough, the horse's front end has to move.

So you don't use your legs to move the horse at this point?

No. I want a colt to learn to depend on the rein. Even though I position my body in the posture that allows me to easily push him with my outside leg, I want this softness to come and the movement to come from the rein and not necessarily because I am helping him with my legs. This is the mental part. I want the horse in time to understand what I am trying to get him to do. I want him to know how to respond to get the release.

If I take his nose and then kind of help him with my leg, I can make him understand quicker, but I am giving him a little bit of a crutch, too. And this is simple stuff, so I don't want to give him the crutch. I want to let him work this out on his own. Later, when I add the ingredient of leg pressure, it then has its own meaning. The only time my leg comes into this picture is if the colt stops and stands still. He must move forward.

If a really hardheaded young colt doesn't lean in that direction, but insists on taking off the other way, what do you do?

I just sit there and hold him and let him go do whatever. I am riding him in the round pen. He can't get away from me. I don't care if I have his nose pulled all the way around to my knee and he is going off the other direction. I just lock down, sit there and hold the rein. I am not going to turn him loose until he releases and gives to that pressure.

That is why, when I first get on a colt, I do it in the round pen instead of taking him to the pasture. I take him to the pasture pretty quickly, but I want to be in the situation where I don't have to compromise what I'm telling a horse because of the surroundings.

I don't care if it takes 15 minutes in the pen. I want to sit there and hang on to him because if I release the rein, I'm training him to go the other way. If he leans on my hand really hard and I give that release, he learns that if he leans hard enough, I turn him loose. If he is hardheaded from the start, then he really is going to get stubborn if I let that happen. The important thing is to set up my situation and be smart enough about these horses so that I don't allow that scenario to unfold. I always need to control the situation so that I always maintain the upper hand.

In Summary

- Basic number one is developing softness from side to side in the horse. That softness comes like the links in a chain, from the horse's head through the shoulders. The beginning of number one is lateral movement with the head. The completion of number one is a lateral move with the foot. Then the horse associates softness with direction, with movement.

- Basic number one's cue is picking up the rein and holding steady pressure until the horse responds by both giving his head and taking a lateral step.

- Basic number one is not complete until that horse responds to a suggestion of the cue. Until the response is mastered to that high degree, I don't continue to basic number two.

No matter how many skills and maneuvers a horse has mastered while maturing, exercises to ensure lateral softness, basic number one, remain a part of the riding program.

ROSS HECOX

"Collecting a horse means... pulling his frame together so he is in an advantageous position to perform any maneuver."

10

Basic Number Two: Breaking at the Poll

By mastering the first basic lesson, the horse is now soft from side to side and has learned to yield to lateral pressure with no resistance. He's ready for the next step.

Now I teach him to break at or be soft in the poll. This is basic number two — collection. Collecting a horse means gathering this horse, pulling his frame together so he is in an advantageous position to perform any maneuver. I do this by setting a barrier with my hands and squeezing him forward with my legs. These things put him in a position where his nose is vertical, his rear end is underneath his body, and he moves quietly in a "ready" position. Just like the tennis player's "ready stance," this position allows the horse to move forward efficiently.

I've taught the horse not to resist the pressure from one rein or the other and to give to the side in the direction of the pressure. Now I can show him another direction to give, and this advances our conversation so the horse begins to respond with other parts of his body.

You might think of basic number two as a step that really helps clarify to the horse that he can have different, simultaneous signals for his body and for his head and neck.

The Second Basic

To ask for basic number two, you begin from a standstill position and, using your elbows, set a barrier with the reins in your hands. Then, using pressure from both legs, ask the horse to move forward into the barrier.

It's critical to understand that when you set this barrier with your hands, you push the horse to walk into the barrier, but you never are pulling on the horse's head. Be sure to lock your elbows or even brace your wrists against the front of the saddle to ensure that your hands stay steady.

Now, with your legs, push the horse up to that barrier. The goal is for the horse to step up there, but be soft in the poll. He collects himself and drives forward from behind without any resistance.

Collection, the second basic, is an important building block that is so necessary to perform advanced maneuvers well.
ROSS HECOX

To teach a horse collection, you must set a barrier with your reins and use your legs to drive your horse forward. Then give him time to figure out how to find the release.

ROSS HECOX

The Initial Reality

In the beginning that collection, as just described, is not going to happen because this second basic is confusing and foreign to the horse. He lets you set that barrier, but when you use both legs, his head and neck come up, and he pulls on your hands.

The conversation might go something like this one:

"Please give to pressure on the reins." (You pick up on reins.)

"I've always just had to give from side to side, but I can sort of do this." (The horse drops his head.)

"Now move forward into the barrier" (You add pressure with your legs, pushing the horse forward.)

"You're nuts. I can't do both. I can either stop or go. Not both. Let me go!" (The horse stops altogether.)

The Second Lesson

When you try to collect the horse with basic number two and the horse pulls on your hands, you have to teach him just like you did when educating him on basic number one. You hold what you have by keeping the hands steady; you also let the pressure that forces the horse into the hackamore or bridle and makes him soft come from your legs. The really important thing about using your legs:

You must learn to use them without conscious thought.

It's also important to remember that this second basic is strenuous for the horse to perform. If you're holding with your hands and clenching with your legs, and basic number two just isn't getting any better, you need to look for a reason to release the horse and let him relax his neck. If not, his neck can cramp. Five minutes is about the most you have before you take a chance of muscle-cramping. The pain from that works against what you are trying to accomplish with the horse.

Remember: Pain plus fear plus adrenalin gives you a fighting situation, rather than a learning situation with the horse seeking the release point. Pushing the horse past that point makes him to dread basic number two, so the next time you ask for collection he's afraid to let himself be put in that position.

Resistance, Understanding, Release

If I just set that barrier with my hands, the horse stands still. I have to set the barrier, and then put pressure on the horse with my legs. At first, I just put the calves of both legs against the horse's sides and push. If nothing happens, then I lift my heels a little bit and touch with the rowels of my spurs. Generally, that is when a green colt lifts his head and

When initially introduced to the second basic, it's not unusual for a horse to resist by dropping the head behind the vertical...
ROSS HECOX

... or by elevating the head with the nose pushed ahead of the vertical.
ROSS HECOX

shows some resistance. When I get that resistance, I hold what I have with my hands and push more with my legs.

This is very difficult for people whose legs are not conditioned to exert this kind of pressure. It's hard to push that much, but you have to set the barrier and then push and lift and push. You don't release the horse until he stops resisting.

The following point also is really important, just as it is with basic number one. When you are getting all kinds of resistance, the horse is trying to turn his neck upside down, and you are holding for all you're worth,

117

The critical thing is that you give that release just as soon as the horse softens through the poll.
ROSS HECOX

That release is so important, no matter if you're riding a snaffle-bit horse in the pen or a hackamore horse in the pasture.
ROSS HECOX

shoving the horse forward with your legs. But when that horse says, "Okay," and gets soft, you must pitch that slack to him. Drop your hands, drop that slack and give that horse an immediate release.

Think of this conversation:

"Let's collect." (You pick up the reins and squeeze with both your legs.)

"Wait. I don't understand. I don't like this." (The horse resists, jerks up his head and then stops entirely.)

"Just try to understand. Move forward into the bridle." (You continue to enforce the barrier and increase pressure with your legs.)

"Stop it. I don't understand." (The horse pulls on the bridle and barely moves forward.)

"Keep trying." (You don't change your hand position and keep pressuring with both legs, asking for forward motion.)

"I've got to get away from this pressure." (The horse continues to pull, bumping the bridle and swishing his tail, and then suddenly drops his head.)

"That's right. You did the right thing!" (Pressure from your hands and legs immediately is released.)

Next, walk the horse around a little bit to let him relax, then ask him to collect again. You probably get that same reaction. He bows up and really shoves on your hands, but then probably softens and gives to get the release a lot quicker the second time. When he does, throw that slack to him. Do the same things again and the softening and collection probably come even a little quicker the third time.

The next day you might have to go through the same initial process again at first. What's important is that you do these things exactly the same way every time. Sit in the middle of your saddle, set the barrier with your hands and push with your legs. When you get the right response, you give your release. That release happens quicker and quicker each time until, when you set that barrier and your pant legs are against the horse's belly, he softens and there is no resistance.

As with basic number one, this softening through the poll develops over a period of time until you can get that response you want every time. Then you take the basic number two to the next level.

The Next Level

When a horse is to the point that every time I lay my legs on him he responds softly,

Initially when changing gaits from a trot to a lope, asking for collection seems like starting all over again, as a horse typically resists framing up and softening through the poll.
ROSS HECOX

However, it seldom takes long for the horse to figure out that collection can result in that same release at a lope that the horse already has discovered at the walk and the trot.
ROSS HECOX

I am going to ask him to hold that collection a little longer than he has been. I drive him forward and walk him around a few steps, then give him a release; then I gather him again and walk around a few more steps, and give him another release. I want to keep

Q&A: Basic Number Two

What happens if you start working in basic number two before the horse is solid on basic number one?

First of all, if you try to teach basic number two before you have number one solid, you get more resistance because the mental acquiescence that comes from a perfectly mastered basic number one is not there. Also, if you try to get the poll soft before you get the softness side to side, you get too deep. In other words, the horse then has a tendency to bend more at the base of the neck than bend the whole neck, and he can learn to get behind the bit.

Does the horse have to be really solid at a walk before going to a trot?

Yes, you get a horse solid at a walk before going to a trot, and solid at a trot before advancing to a lope. At any gait, there is a progression with three stages: First, you ask the horse to do what you want. Next, you ask him to hold that position. Then, you expect him to maintain it on his own. You make him responsible.

What do you mean by remodeling the horse's physical structure?

You are working with the horse's physical development. When you put him in the bridle and shove him forward with your legs, you are stretching muscles that the horse hasn't had stretched before. You put him in a position that is foreign to him and make him hold that position.

As you go along, you stretch the horse's top line and actually physically change the characteristics of his neck to a certain degree. You strengthen the top line and you cause the underline to atrophy a little bit.

I can't do these things in a week or two; it takes time. That is why I start with 2-year-olds. I hope to have this collection by December of a horse's 3-year-old year. If things are done by then, it is because the horse has pretty good conformation to start.

Although I do physically change the muscle structure, there is not anything I can do about the horse's bone structure. If a horse's neck comes out of his shoulders and sticks up in the air like an ostrich, this type of work is not going to change him a whole lot although there can be some improvement. But if a horse has a good neck to start with, the work definitely enhances the neck.

When you become comfortable and familiar with this basic number two work, you get to the point that you can look at a horse standing in a stall and pretty much tell if he's soft in the bridle or not, just because of the way his muscle coverage looks. If you see a horse that's thick and muscled under the neck, chances are he's not soft in the bridle.

Remember: You don't start on basic number two until you have basic number one exactly the way you want it to be. And you don't start on basic number three until you have perfected basic number two because each step builds on the one that precedes it. Everything is a matter of progression.

Now with basics number one and number two, you have softness from side to side, responsiveness, and softness in this horse's poll. You have tremendous control of this horse's front end.

Next, you have to get control of the horse's rear end. You're ready for basic number three.

A horse that's way behind the vertical typically bends more at the base of the neck, often the result of moving to basic two's collection work before the first basic of lateral flexion has been mastered.

ROSS HECOX

developing that soft response until I can walk, trot or lope the horse, do whatever I want, and keep him in that collected position.

From there I progress to teaching that horse to round and collect, and maintain this collected position on his own. Actually, I'm almost remodeling this horse's physical structure. I stretch the muscles at the top of his neck, over his back and down through his hips. He develops muscle along the top of his neck and even can become softer underneath his neck.

How easy these things are for this horse depends entirely on his conformation. If he has a good top line, is strong through his back and hips, and has a nice neck that comes out of his shoulders right, then collection is easy for him. And it is not going to be much of a struggle. If he is a hollow-backed, low-withered horse with a high neck-set, it is tough for him to collect; you are going to have to work on it and work on it. Remember: The horse learns through repetition. Keep repeating these cues, exactly the same way, every time.

The steps in teaching basic number two are as specific as those laid out for basic number one. First, you get the horse to accept being collected. Then you get him to accept maintaining that position. Finally, he learns to be responsible for maintaining that position on his own.

In Summary

- Basic number two is collection. That means pushing the horse forward into the barrier created with the bridle until that horse breaks in the poll, staying soft with no resistance.

- Basic number two's cues are the rider setting a barrier with both reins at the same time the rider's legs squeeze to drive the horse forward.

- Basic number two is not complete until the horse responds to the suggestion of those cues. Until this basic is mastered to that high degree, I don't continue to basic number three.

This second principle of collection is much the same with a hackamore as it is with the snaffle; you set the barrier with your reins and drive your horse forward until he's moving in frame.
ROSS HECOX

Before long a hackamore horse figures out how to find that release; then collection becomes a matter of maintenance with your horse learning to hold that frame for gradually longer periods of time.
ROSS HECOX

"Basic number three is a really important part of getting this horse broke to ride so I can... teach him the advanced maneuvers."

11

Basic Number Three: Moving Away From Leg Pressure

At this point, I've established some pretty clear methods of communicating with the horse. He's confident, never startled when I pick up the reins to signal him. He trusts that when I make a movement or put pressure on him in some way that I'm asking him to do something. He's not defensive because I've never done anything to make him apprehensive about his work sessions. Since he's developed this confidence and has polished his basic number one and basic number two skills to a very high degree, he's ready to move to a new level.

The Third Basic

Basic number three gives me control of the horse's rear end by teaching him to respond and yield to leg pressure. I want the horse to move his body away when I lay a leg on him. He does that in motion, going forward, moving ahead. That's

why it is so important that basic number two is as perfect as I can get it before I start working on number three.

To introduce this third basic to the horse, I ride the horse up and into the bridle, putting him in a collected position. I hold that position with both legs and both reins. I should feel no resistance, no pressure. Now I take pressure off one of my legs by moving it away from the horse's side while I push a little harder with my other leg. I want the horse to move his hip over for me.

The Initial Reality

The first time I do basic number three on a 2-year-old, I am going to get some resistance, and my basic number two response might break down a little bit. The colt might pick up his neck a little and try to break through the barrier of the bridle

The better you develop your horse's understanding of basics one and two—without causing apprehension—the more easily you can introduce number three and move the hindquarters.

Whenever you introduce anything new, a horse's first reaction often is to show resistance by elevating his neck and head.
ROSS HECOX

Minimize tail-swishing, a common response in learning this skill, by releasing pressure quickly when the horse makes an honest effort.
ROSS HECOX

or hackamore, but I just hold and hold and hold, with both my hands and that one leg. If I want the horse to move to the right, I ride him up into the bridle, take my right leg off the horse and push on the horse with my left leg. If he doesn't move, I just continue to hold and continue to push. But as soon as he moves that hip, I take my leg off his side.

Your conversation goes something like this:

"Please collect." (You pick up the reins and apply leg pressure.)

"That's easy." (The horse moves into the collected position of a perfect basic number two, ready for whatever comes next.)

"Now, let's move your hip over to the right." (You maintain the barrier with those reins, remove your right leg pressure, and continue pushing with your left leg.)

"Wait, I don't understand!" (The horse swishes his tail, speeds up, and pushes against bridle in confusion.)

The Third Lesson

Now, if I try basic number three and the colt completely forgets basic number two, lifting his neck and breaking up through the bridle, rather than collecting, that means basic number two isn't as good as I thought it was. It's time for us to review number two.

Once that's done and I am ready to try basic number three again, I repeat the same procedure. I remember to cue the horse to move his hindquarters by pushing with my leg. I always apply that pressure gradually, starting with the calf, then my lower leg and then the rowel of the spur. If I always use my leg

Apply pressure, for example, with the left leg to move your horse's hips to the right and open your right leg to give him a place to go.
ROSS HECOX

Develop a quiet, responsive horse by cueing for basic number three and then giving the horse time to figure out and understand what you want.
ROSS HECOX

that way, eventually, the horse responds to my lower leg, then to a soft movement of my calf. I remember to keep my leg pressure steady and use a slow, deliberate push, not a kick.

This time, the conversation is better:

"Please collect." (You pick up the reins, and apply leg pressure with both legs.)

"That's easy." (The horse moves into the collected position of a perfect basic number two, his body in frame.)

"Now, let's move your hip over to the right." (You maintain rein pressure, remove your right leg pressure, and continue pushing with your left leg.)

"I don't know exactly what's happening, but I know I have to keep myself collected." (The horse continues to move forward into the barrier, swishing his tail, and tries to speed up.)

"Just try." (You continue using your cues and increase pressure with your left leg.)

"I've got to move away from that thing in my side." (The horse moves hip slightly to the right—an effort to respond.)

"That's right!" (You release the pressure immediately.)

Resistance, Understanding, Release

One common mistake at this point is to bend the horse's head to the inside while pushing his hip out. I prefer to keep his head aimed forward.

In the beginning, as soon as I feel the slightest obedience or movement away from my leg, I am going to take off my leg pressure. But I work on this basic at a walk until

125

Keep things simple. Apply pressure with your left leg and open the door with your right leg to move your horse's hindquarters to the right, or vice versa.
ROSS HECOX

Ideally your horse's front end continues on the same path, as the hindquarters move to track right of that path, as shown in this example.
ROSS HECOX

I can give pressure with my leg and the horse moves his hip with no resistance at all.

Three is, without a doubt, the toughest basic to teach because it depends so much on having mastered the other two basics, so keep reviewing them. With number three, it's normal for the horse to swish his tail, and even the best colts often give a lot of resistance to your hands. The best way to shorten that period of resistance is to consistently and immediately release the horse from pressure as soon as you get a correct response.

Sometimes, for example, a young stallion feels your leg for the first time and he just leans right into you. If he does, press harder and hold the rowel steady against the colt. Don't kick him, but you might move your leg up and down to roll that rowel against the horse's side until he finally moves away. Then release your leg.

The Next Level

When the horse moves his hip without resistance, I begin to build on that response, trying to get the horse to hold his hip in position a little longer each time. At first, as soon as I get movement, I give him a release, but now I want to develop this response to the point the horse can hold the position. Then, in time, I can be riding along with the horse collected, take one leg off the horse, push with my other leg, and the horse's hip moves over and away from the leg pressure. And the horse just keeps right on going without deviating from the line or path we started riding.

Dressage people call this third maneuver a leg yield, but I just call it moving the hip over. Basic number three is such a really important part of getting this horse broke to ride, so I then can go ahead and teach him the advanced maneuvers.

Q&A: Basic Number Three

How exactly do you cue for basic number three? Where exactly does the leg go and how far back along the horse's side?

I just move the one leg away from the horse's side and push stronger with the other leg. For example, if I am asking the horse to move his hip to the right, I shift my weight to my left hip, pushing with that left leg as I move my right leg away from the colt to open a way, a direction, for him to move. I am not athletic enough to have three or four positions for my leg. If I was, and I sold that horse to someone who had shorter legs, I don't want things to be so complicated that the new owner can't ride the horse. I just want to make things so that when I take my leg off one side of the horse and push with the leg on other side, the horse's rear end moves.

Do you hold the horse's body straight?

Yes. I am definitely controlling the horse's front end with my hands as I ride the horse forward. I want his front end to stay on the same line, the same plane. I want just the rear end to move to the side.

I want to build this third skill to the point that I can go a hundred yards with my leg on the horse and he travels in a straight line, willingly and freely. Once he can do that at a walk, I try it at a trot. Once the horse can do number three at a trot, I try three at a lope.

If, when you increase the speed, the colt is resistant in your hands, his nose goes out with his back hollow, it's time to back down and go a notch slower in speed. Remember: Just because a colt moves his hip a few times walking doesn't mean he's ready to try moving his hip at a lope. Go at his pace, not yours.

When the colt can maintain basic number three at a lope for however long he's asked, and he has mastered basics one and two to a very high level, he has a great set of basic skills. But even though he's mastered these skills, I do not stop reviewing them and polishing them. They become a part of the horse's daily regimen of exercise for the rest of his life.

By teaching your horse to move a hip and maintain collected forward motion, you develop another building block for smoothly performed advanced maneuvers, such as canter departures.
ROSS HECOX

A smooth, quiet canter departure comes easily once your horse has mastered basic skill number three.
ROSS HECOX

The front view reflects the same cues for a right-lead lope—weight on the left hip, pressure from the left leg and no pressure on the right leg, or just the opposite when asking for a left lead.
ROSS HECOX

In Summary

- Basic number three is the horse moving away from leg pressure. Initially, you teach that move and, as you perfect number three, the colt learns to maintain that position until you release—and at the different gaits.

- Basic number three is cued for by first asking for basic number two, then releasing the pressure with one leg while maintaining the pressure with the other leg until the colt moves his hip away from that pressure.

- Basic number three is not complete until the horse moves on the suggestion of the cue. Until number three is mastered to that high degree, I don't consider the colt ready to move to advanced maneuvers.

Section Six

Advanced Conversation

In this section I show how the three simple basics in combination with one other make teaching advanced maneuvers to a horse not only easier, but also with a much higher ratio of success than some might expect. Because these three basics have been so thoroughly taught to the horse, I am able to break any complex lesson down into simple parts, or steps. As I teach a horse the advanced skills, if there is any confusion on the horse's part, I can go back to the basics to help him successfully perform an advanced maneuver.

12

Circles and Lead Changes

Certainly by this point, I have loped my horse in a circle. But it is only after I have completed all three basics and I am totally satisfied with how the horse performs these basics that I begin formal and structured circle training. It is very important that a horse have this formal training because without it, when a horse is shown in competition, he soon deteriorates into pulling this way, leaning that way, speeding up, rushing through lead changes—a total mess.

Even though I am very particular about lead departures, I am not overly concerned about them at this point. If my colt wants to trot several steps before he picks up a lead, that's fine. That is far more acceptable than having him bolt into a lope, and then having to slow him down.

Ultimately I want this colt to be very relaxed and step quietly into the desired lead. For this reason, I don't want to begin formal circle training as soon as the colt comes out of the barn. Instead, a 20- to 30-minute trail ride while reviewing the basics can be ideal. Lacking this, perhaps a half-hour on the walker might accomplish the same thing.

As with circling, a smooth lead departure is the result of mastering basics number two and number three—poll flexion and control of the horse's hip.

Those also are the two basics necessary for successful lead changes. Obviously, the better my horse has mastered basics two and three, the more easily I can advance him to the next level and develop smooth, quiet lead changes.

Circle Position

The first phase of my formal circle training is circle position, teaching the horse how to maintain his position while traveling in a circle. In order to accomplish this, I use a combination of basics number two and basic number three—collection and moving the hip or, in this case, stabilizing the horse's hip.

I begin by crossing my reins and holding them in the hand on the side in the direction I am going to circle. In other words, right hand equals right circle and left hand for a left circle. That's what I typically do although in some of the photos I'm shown riding two-handed with a hackamore.

Then, I set my barrier with my hands, as described in basic two, and push my horse into a right-lead lope, using a slightly stronger left leg. Again, if he wants to trot several steps before picking up the correct lead, that is okay.

Long before it's time to ask a horse for speed in competition, it's necessary to establish position and rate.

Although I'm using two hands on a hackamore in some of the photos, I often cross the bridle reins and hold them in one hand when working on a horse's circle position.

ROSS HECOX

After he picks up the lope, I hold my barrier for a few strides and then slowly drop my rein hand. As long as the horse stays in the circle position, maintaining the circle, I leave my hand down.

If the horse speeds up, leans to the outside or leans to the inside, I pick up my hand smoothly, but not too quickly, press with my left leg, maintain contact for three or four strides, and then slowly drop my hand again. It is through this constant correction-and-release process that the horse learns what is expected of him. If I constantly hold him in the desired position without the release, he soon becomes uncomfortable and wants out of the position. It is only through the correction-and-release process that I am able to train a solid, reliable horse that I confidently can show in the circle.

Using the Legs

At this time, you must consider the role that your legs play in teaching a horse to maintain the circle position. As discussed above, when there is any deviation on the part of the horse, you set the barrier and press with your left or outside leg. Although this is true, it is applicable only in the situation where the horse is fading or pulling to the outside of the circle.

In the situation when the horse pulls to the inside of the circle, you must do exactly what you've been doing with one added ingredient. While your left leg maintains control of

the hip, your right leg bumps the horse at the area just behind the cinch. This bumping should almost be like you are trying to drive a wooden peg through the horse, using your stirrup as the hammer. Once the horse moves to the outside and is following the original circle again, stop bumping and release your right leg and the barrier.

The reason it is so important to maintain steady pressure with the outside leg is that, without that pressure, the horse can drop off-lead behind or change leads altogether even though a colt is not ready to change leads yet. It is vitally important that he does not develop bad habits at the point.

Also in this scenario, the horse might think this bumping with the inside leg is a signal

Redirecting a horse to the outside, for example, requires both legs—one to hold him on lead and the other to push the horse over to travel another path.

ROSS HECOX

to increase his speed. If this is the case, slow down the horse to a trot or even a walk, but continue bumping until he is on track in the circling position. Then pick up the lead you started and continue loping for a period of time. You might have to reduce the horse's speed to a slow gait each time his speed-up occurs, but eventually you are able to bump him out of the circle without the horse increasing his speed.

If your horse tends to speed up and wants to run, instead of exhausting him until he is unable to go fast, just gradually pull him down to a walk. Walk four or five circles, and then lope him again. Each time he wants to go fast, make him walk. Spend as much time as you need. But before you finish that riding session, make sure the horse has loped four or five circles quietly before you put him away.

One thing that always helps me, when I am working on circles at this stage, is dragging my arena so there are no tracks in it. Then, I lope a circle, and can keep following right in my horse's tracks.

If you drag your riding area, keep working on those circles until you have a two- or three-foot-wide perfectly round path that you are following. This gives you a constant reference point and can be a useful tool in successfully making round circles and maintaining your horse's position.

Redirecting to the Inside

At this point, I have loped circles at only one speed, which is a comfortable ground-covering gait. The colt is relaxed; he is obedient and consistently follows the circle with a minimum of slight corrections. Now it is time to add the second phase of my circle training, which is teaching the colt to guide from an indirect rein, or neck-rein.

Although some of these photographs have been shot in the pen, I very seldom begin this training in an enclosed arena. I prefer to start in a large open field when the ground is dry and I am able to ride at least about a hundred yards or more in a straight line. This allows the colt to think for a few seconds between my guiding exercises and provides him with a reason for what I am doing.

If an arena is the only place you have to ride, the same results can be accomplished. However, you proceed much slower, and the chance for confusing your colt is much greater than in an open field.

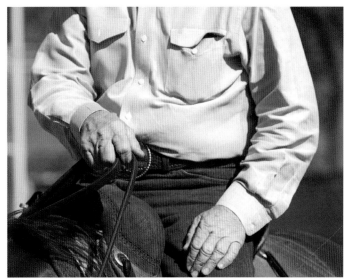

When redirecting a horse to the left, I often use my right hand to stroke the right rein on the horse's neck and, when necessary, can use my left hand to reinforce my request, or vice versa when redirecting a horse to the right.
ROSS HECOX

Although redirecting a horse 45 degrees inside the circle might seem awkward at first, timing is everything. Redirection works best when the hind feet are underneath the horse's body and the release is given the second the horse changes direction.
ROSS HECOX

As is the case with the introduction of any new thing, I don't begin my guiding exercises on a Monday morning. I generally wait until midweek when the horse is doing everything I have taught him so far and with a workman-like attitude.

I begin my guiding exercise by quietly loping the horse in a long straight line and on his left lead. I hold my reins in my right hand with one finger between them, as I would if I were showing. It is very important at this time that the colt is loping quietly and with some slack in the bridle reins. Then I slowly and smoothly pick up my right rein hand, rubbing the slack of the right rein against the horse's neck, but I absolutely do not let the right rein get tight.

At this point, the colt probably does not move in the desired direction, toward the left. When he doesn't, I continue to hold that right rein although still not tightly. When the hind feet are underneath the horse's body, I pick up the left rein with my left hand, again very smoothly, and pull him to about a 45-degree angle, at the same time bumping with my right foot. As soon as the colt makes that angle change, I release with the left hand and drop my right hand to hold the rein in a position just in front of the saddle horn.

It is very important that doing this does not scare the horse. As the rider, you must use a lot of judgment about how hard to pull and how hard to bump the horse. Your goal is not to pull his nose so he bends his neck, but to pick up his front end and set it down at the 45-degree angle.

If your horse gets scared and wants to pick up speed, immediately drop him back to a walk and let him relax. Walk around. Then, again lope him in the left lead and try the guiding exercise. Eventually, even by the end of the first session, he reacts to the slight lift and rub of the right rein against his neck by redirecting himself in a fairly acceptable manner.

After redirecting the horse to the left for a while—seven, eight, even 10 times—start doing the same exercise to the right. Change hands, with the reins now in your left hand and one finger between the reins. Now lope the horse on the right lead and repeat the redirection process doing exactly what you did when going to the left. From now on this exercise should be a part of your daily riding routine.

Redirecting to the Outside

Now that you have a good concept of guiding your horse to the inside of the circle, you must address guiding him to the outside. Begin by loping on the left lead, rein in the left hand, sitting on your right hip, with your right leg and calf close to the horse's ribs. Because of your previous session, constantly guiding the horse to the inside of the circle, your colt probably is leaning to the inside a little bit. Remember, you really are riding in straight lines and angles, not just loping circles.

Now lope your horse along your straight line and this time rub the left rein up your horse's neck—and you probably get no response. Then, when the horse's hind feet are on the ground, pull the right rein and bump with the left leg, sending the horse 45 degrees to the right. The only difference between guiding the horse into the circle and out from the circle is that when you're guiding out, you must press your outside leg, in

When a horse's shoulder drops even slightly inside, to the left, for example, it's time to redirect the horse to the right.
ROSS HECOX

this case your right leg, with some authority or the horse might change leads. Repeat this guiding-out process seven to 10 times.

Then, let your colt stop and catch his breath. It is very important, with all of these advanced maneuvers, to provide little breaks after a few minutes of work. These rests not only allow a colt an opportunity to catch his breath, but also give him a chance to think.

Now start on the right lead, reins in your right hand, one finger between them, and repeat exactly the above process. Remember: It is vitally important to be sitting on your left hip and pressing harder with your left calf when you guide the horse out of the circle.

Circling at the Next Level

Once the colt or horse understands the basic concept of guiding, which should take only a few days, you can now start mixing up things while continuing to travel those long straight lines, sometimes guiding in and sometimes guiding out until the colt is responsive to your cues. Instead of anticipating, he lopes long straight lines, waits for you to give him the lifting or rubbing cue, and then responds obediently.

At this time, now try to make a 20-degree change of direction, then a 10-degree change. Make several of these, and then make another big 45-degree change. Do not lose sight of the goal, which is to get this colt to change his direction of travel when you lift your hand in either direction, but without the horse changing leads, picking up speed, picking up his head or doing anything other than the simple change of direction. From this point, a review of directional changes becomes part of your routine during each ride.

Now let's go back to the discussion about circles. It should be obvious that when your horse guides lightly, softly and obediently in each direction that loping a circle is easy.

Typically when first rubbing the left rein against the horse's neck, to redirect him to the outside, there is little or no response.

ROSS HECOX

That's the time to redirect the horse obviously by using the right rein and bumping him to the right with your left leg.

ROSS HECOX

However, when a horse is training in a fairly tight or small area, the urge to pull in one direction or another is very strong. Normally the horse tends to follow the path of least resistance, which is traveling a shorter distance by virtue of a smaller circle.

In the case of a horse that pulls to the outside of the circle, almost always a fear of changing leads or a fear of what is at the end of the arena is the problem. In any case, you must deal with these fears by whatever means necessary.

Training a horse to circle in this program has stair-step phases for increasing his skills. However, when you move from one phase to another, it is important to note that you should never neglect your previous training. That's because when you begin to work on guiding the horse, doing so might wreck your horse maintaining circle position. If this happens, go back and review circle position for a few days; then try guiding your horse again. These reviews might happen several times but in the end the parts blend into the same, smooth maneuver.

Speed Control

When I have the other two parts of the circle program firmly in place—circle position and guiding—then I introduce the fundamentals of speed control to the horse.

As in presenting anything new in my program, I don't begin working on speed control on Monday morning after the horse has had a day off from his routine. Instead, I plan to introduce speed control the middle of the week when the horse is working well and doing everything I ask.

After the horse is warmed up and I've reviewed all the basics, I lope a few slow circles in a nice, easy, ground-covering lope. Then, in the circle, I lean forward, run my hand forward on the horse's neck and move my legs slightly back into the ribcage. I cluck to the horse and ask him to increase his speed.

In the beginning, he can be a little hesitant because I've stayed at a slow speed in circles prior to this point. The horse probably starts to speed up, but if he doesn't, I bump him with my legs—without spurs—until he does increase his speed.

In bumping the horse to get him to speed up, it's important to remember to do so with your legs—not your heels—and do not kick him with the spur or roll the spur up and down his side. The reason: If you use a spur to speed up the horse, the spur also causes him to speed up when you ask the horse to move his hip in other maneuvers. Spurs are much more effective tools in moving the horse's body and cueing, so you never want a horse to think that spurs mean for him to speed up.

Finally, after being asked to increase his speed, my horse lengthens his stride and goes a little faster than before. I ride two or three circles at this fast speed. And that fast speed is not as fast as he ultimately goes; it's fast for him at this stage of training.

Then I ask for the opposite—a decrease in speed. All speed control depends on my position so when I sit deeply and heavily in the saddle and put my hand back in its original, right-in-front-of-the-saddle-horn position, that means for the horse to slow his speed. I have my heels under my spine, sitting deep in my saddle and with no leg pressure, which is completely different from what I did when asking the horse to go fast.

When he feels this change in my body position, my horse probably decreases his speed, but if he doesn't, I lift the reins one time to let him know it's okay to slow his speed. If the horse doesn't respond then, I lift the slack out of the reins, engage his mouth and continue to pull a little stronger and stronger until he hits a couple of trotting steps and comes down to a walk. Then I relax the reins again and let the horse walk.

This correction is not done in a harsh way at all. I'm just letting the horse know that it's all right to slow down now. It's almost like saying, "When I relax, it's okay for you to relax!" I want him in the mindset that he responds completely to my position and that I do not allow him to go fast when he and I are in the slow position.

Working on speed control is a critical time for a horse. The last thing you want to do is to have a horse running because he is scared. The only goal at this time is to let him know that he should go faster when you lean forward and go slowly when you relax and sit down in the saddle. In time, the horse's response should become such a habit and so ingrained in his mind that, even if he is very fresh, he slows down when you sit down and relax.

One thing about this speed-control exercise I want to make very clear. When making the downward transition, I always go fast, then go slow—and then walk. Many people I have observed go fast, then go slow, and then go fast again. If that is done very often, the horse begins to not slow down as much as he should. Especially in the beginning, going slowly and getting back to the walk is something the horse perceives as the release point or his reward.

So I walk for a few minutes and then I step the horse into a lope again. I want a standard slow, easy, flowing lope for a couple of circles before I again lean forward, run my hand forward over his neck and, with my legs in his belly, ask him to go fast. If the horse doesn't pick up speed, I bump him with my legs and send him fast around a couple of circles. Then I sit down, relax my feet away from his belly, put my hand in front of the saddle horn and allow him to go slowly. If the horse doesn't slow, I pull him down to a walk. Throughout, I emphasize that one position means to go fast, and the other position means to go slowly.

Horses respond to this phase of training differently. Some are edgy and when you ask them to increase speed; they'd rather run. Those are the ones you bring to a walk and walk for a long time.

On that first day do these things two or three times in each direction. Think of this as an introduction. Some horses learn to respond the first day. With others you don't see much progress the first day, but maybe they respond the second day. The more consistent you are in doing these things, the more consistent the horse becomes about speed control.

Repeat this process each day until the horse goes slowly when you ask him. If he doesn't slow down, pull him down. When he doesn't go fast, keep after him until he does. Through these repetitions your cues become clear signals to go fast or to go slowly, and the horse learns and obeys those cues.

It's essential to understand that a little inconsistency on your part can be a big inconsistency for the horse. You're trying to teach him a very exacting science. These inconsistencies include running your hand way up behind the horse's ears one time, for example, then another time having your hand midway down his mane or the third time having your hand forward only three or four inches. It's the same for your legs if they're way back along a horse's sides one time, then in the middle the next. Those are careless inconsistencies that a horse reads and picks up on easily. These inconsistencies are things you might not pay attention to, but they make a huge difference to the horse. Be precise; understand that a cue is not the same to a horse unless the cue is

Ask for speed by leaning forward, moving the rein hand up the horse's neck, and dropping your legs back along the horse's sides. Then allow the horse to travel fast with that longer stride for a distance.
ROSS HECOX

To rate the horse and reduce speed, sit back deeply into the saddle, moving the rein hand back to its original position. If necessary for the horse's understanding, lift the reins or even bring the horse to a trot.
ROSS HECOX

exactly the same each time it is used. Then the horse understands you.

Some horses get a little panicky with the speed. They are a little scared of the running, so it becomes counterproductive. That's why I don't "chase" horses, asking them to go faster for a while until they want to slow down. That works for some but not for all, so it's something I no longer use in my program.

Almost all horses accelerate to a certain degree but there are extremes each way; some horses don't run and some don't slow down. It's important to understand that good horses can be at both ends of spectrum. You just have to spend the time working with each horse as an individual.

Speed Beyond the Circle

Once my horse's responses for speed are established in the circles, I can apply these same principles in other places. After I get a horse working well in the circles, I use speed control, for example, around the outside of the track or the arena. I'm 10 to 15 feet off that rail and increase speed on the straightaway, then slow down near the end. The horse has to learn to accelerate and decelerate in places other than the circles.

The essence of this training is the end result—having a horse that can think and be responsive to your cues at any speed.

Competing in any event, you need to be able to control a horse's speed by cues, rather than having to hold and pull him down through brute force. No one enjoys riding a horse like that, but everyone likes the horse that is immediately responsive to the rider's hands. When you pick up the reins, your horse slows or stops.

These are things that Ray Hunt told us 30 years ago when he talked about putting life into the horse and drawing the life out of a horse. What he meant is what I'm discussing here—giving a horse a cue to go fast and a cue to go slow.

When my horse is doing nice downward transitions, speeding up when asked and appearing comfortable with all the above, I begin experimenting with finding the speed at which the horse looks the best. Just because a horse can run at top speed in a circle doesn't mean that his most pleasing appearance is at that speed. Perhaps one or two notches below that speed, the horse takes on a pretty profile. Maybe when a particular

A horse needs to understand that speed control applies anywhere—in the arena or the pasture.

ROSS HECOX

horse is going as slowly as he can lope, he appears sluggish and draggy. But he can appear bright and alert when moving just a little bit faster.

Taking a look at speed evaluation is best accomplished with a video camera. Video the horse at different speeds—both fast and slow. When you have decided at which speeds the horse looks best, practice riding at those speeds only. When you ask the horse to run fast, he hits that one speed and stays there, and you do the same with the horse at a slow speed. Later, when you present a horse to judges, you want him to work at his optimum speeds.

Walk, Don't Run

In clinics I often see horses that don't want to walk. They take a step or two then move into a trot, pushing on their bits. Or they just jig all the time instead of walking.

There are different reasons the horses do these things but overall they are feeling anxiety. Maybe they've been jump-started by people hanging the slack, then kicking with both legs to launch the horses forward. The horses begin to think that anytime the reins are loose, it must be launch time.

Then you have a horse that's on the muscle all the time—wanting to push on the bridle. He's probably been held since he was a 2-year-old and doesn't know what to do when he's turned loose—except go faster.

You can plan for this correction to take a while for most horses. Start at a walk; cue the horse to go forward and loosen the reins. As soon as he takes a fast step, stop and back him—not in an abusive way—just in a firm way. Horses are so perceptive; don't make this a punishment but a correction. If the horse is on the muscle because he is anxious and perceives this backing as punishment, that increases his desire to get away. It's your job through training to overcome the horse's instinct to run away from anxiety and you do this by building his confidence. It's impossible to instill enough fear that a horse doesn't run.

So you have to learn exact repetition and to pay attention exactly. You can't start this correction and halfway through the session lose your concentration, and then start holding the horse. If you do, then all you have done is tell him you were lying to him and it becomes even harder to build his confidence.

This takes a lot of time. It's your opportunity to learn exact repetition. Even if you do

Correcting a horse that's a little anxious or on the muscle is just that—a correction and not punishment.
ROSS HECOX

things correctly for a week's time, then get frustrated and jerk the reins, you've just gone back to square one.

The good news is that although it might take a while, this retraining formula for the horse works. When the horse improves, remember to work on these things and reinforce them every time you school the horse.

The Collected Lead Departure

A lead departure in its purest form is a combination of basic number two and basic number three. The horse is collected and soft through the poll and moves away from leg pressure. In order to achieve the kind of lead departure that earns points in reining or other types of competition, those two basics have to be highly developed.

I teach the lead departure using those two basics, but long before the basics are mastered enough ask for a lead departure, I am

Although I always cue a young horse for a lead departure just as I do a finished horse, it's okay at first if a green horse trots a few steps—as long as the horse is collected and in frame.

ROSS HECOX

For a right lead, I collect the horse, put my weight to the left, close my left leg on his side and open my right leg so he can move forward in that direction.

ROSS HECOX

already loping the horse. In the beginning, on a colt that has not yet mastered basics number two and three, I ask for the lead departure like I do later, with an outside heel and a collection. After I ask the "grown-up" way, I go ahead and push the colt into a lope. If he trots a few steps before moving into a lope at this point, it's okay. The worst thing I can do is try to make a collected lead departure from a standstill before the colt has developed those basics. That scares and confuses the horse and makes my job difficult.

One of the things I have established to prepare this horse for a lifetime of smooth lead departures: I never allow the horse to step forward without being in a collected position. I always collect the horse, then move forward. I never stop a horse to let him rest, then bump him up to walk over to the fence and talk to someone without first making him collect; then I go forward. If at first I don't collect him before moving forward, I take away from his ability to learn a collected lead departure.

In any circumstances, to walk the horse forward, I pick up on the reins, balance his face to collect him, and then move ahead. Once he's started that forward motion in a collected manner, I can continue to go forward with a loose rein and with no detrimental effects.

So, to ask a horse for a lead departure from a standstill, I collect him, balancing him with my hands. To take a right lead, I put the horse in that collected position while sitting with my weight on the left, outside hip. Then I apply pressure with my left leg as my right leg moves away from the horse's side. That opens a door for him to move in that direction and the horse steps into that lead. Now, if a young horse trots forward a few steps here, that's okay as long as he doesn't challenge basic number two and stays collected.

As I continue to repeat this process, the trotting periods should shorten until they don't exist. If the horse does make a mistake by violating basic number two and crosses the barrier set with my hands, I stop him, back up and do whatever I need to reinforce basic number two until I can collect the horse, apply leg pressure and have him move forward smoothly into a lope.

So what's the difference between basic number three with the horse moving away from leg pressure and what I'm doing when asking for a collected lead departure?

Ultimately the horse trots less and soon can learn to move quickly, quietly and matter-of-factly into a right-lead lope.

ROSS HECOX

Movement. Basic number three is initiated by movement, but a lead departure doesn't start with movement. It starts with a standstill.

It's common to see a person in the show ring do a very exaggerated hip movement prior to the lead departure. I think that shows a lack of confidence in the horse's ability to take the correct lead.

The confident and well-trained horse should have impeccable lead departures that require only subtle cues. He should be able to stand on all four feet and then move into the correct lead, and the movement of his hindquarters should be almost imperceptible to observers.

The Lead Change

The timing of how I change leads on a horse is almost exactly the same timing needed to stop a horse. In other words, as the horse lopes, for example, in the left lead, this horse's front end rolls forward and comes down as his weight shifts onto that leading leg, and both hind feet are being carried up and underneath him. At that point in his stride, there is only one leg on the ground—the leading left front. If I can cue that horse

so that the message to change leads gets to his brain at that particular moment, all he has to do is drop his right hind and front legs to the ground, and he is now loping in the right lead. So the timing for a lead change is as important as the mechanism I use.

If you are inexperienced, before you try to change a lead, take your horse to the pasture and ride along in a slow lope. As your horse lopes and you feel his weight shifting forward on that leading front leg, say, "Now." Continue to do that each time you feel that rolling forward motion when your horse's weight comes down on the leading front leg: "Now. Now. Now." This exercise can help you with timing and learning when to cue the horse for the lead change.

To prepare your horse to change leads, review and emphasize basics two and three. After reinforcing the correct responses, trot your horse forward in a straight line and pick out a target, a tree or a fence post. Trot forward in that straight line and move your horse's hip to the right. As soon as that hip moves right, take your left leg off the horse's side and, with your right leg, move his hip immediately back to the left. If you can trot that horse in a straight line and move his hips

The ideal time to ask a horse for a lead change is when the animal's weight shifts forward to the leading leg just as his two hind feet are leaving the ground.
ROSS HECOX

Although your feet change position and your weight shifts as you ask for the right lead, continue to keep the horse traveling straight, without leaning in either direction.
ROSS HECOX

from left to right and right to left immediately and without any hesitation, worry, or speeding on the horse's part, then you have done a good job on your basic number three. That horse is ready to try a lead change.

I usually say that I know I'm ready to ask the horse for a lead change when I know for a fact that he is going to make that change without a problem. I think this is a wise thing for anyone to ask himself before trying to change leads.

Changing leads is something that I prefer to try outside in a big, open area, as opposed to a small arena, simply because of the space. Outside, I'm loping this horse in a left lead in a nice big circle. Each time, as his body rolls forward to shift onto that leading leg, I am saying, "Now. Now. Now." Of course, since my

horse is loping in the left lead, my weight is on my right hip with my right leg pulled back, toward the horse's flank. I'm not really pressing with a spur but the calf of my right leg is there to support the horse as he goes along in the circle. My left leg is out and away from the horse's body. That body position is like me opening the door for the horse to move in that direction. I am sitting in the proper position, loping along, preparing the horse for the lead change.

Then, I take this horse off the circle and start riding him in a straight line. To change leads, all I need to do is shift my hips. I want to hold the horse's neck and head steady as I slide my weight from my right hip to the left hip and press with my left leg. This causes that horse to move his hip to the right and he

The lead change might not be smooth at first, but it's important not to scare your horse during his initial efforts and to help him figure out what you want him to do.
ROSS HECOX

Following the lead change, it's best to continue loping straight for several strides before resuming the circle. Then your horse doesn't associate the lead change with that change in direction.
ROSS HECOX

should change leads with no hesitation, and keep right on moving in that straight line.

At this point, it is very important that I continue riding on that straight line because I don't want the horse to learn that a lead change and a change of direction are associated in any way at all. I want this horse to be able to change leads on a straight line, in a counter-canter, or wherever I want—and then, after the lead change, wait for me to tell him which direction to go. This is very important for the long-term preservation of the horse, particularly as a show horse if that's what I'm going to do with him. I never want a horse to relate a change of lead to a change in direction as that leads to anticipation.

So now I've changed my horse to a right lead and I continue to lope on this straight line. I'm not going to bend this horse to the right at all; I'm just going to lope him for a hundred yards or so. Then gradually, after riding on this long straight line, I lope the horse to the right and in a circle, and keep loping him several minutes or more before trying to change leads. Again, I don't want to make a big deal about the lead change. I lope my horse around in the right lead for a while until he's relaxed, chilled out, and happy to be out there.

Then I do the same things that I did before, but to the right. I lope a nice big right circle, sitting on my left hip with my left leg pulled back toward the horse's left flank to support him from the outside. My right leg is out away from his body. I straighten my horse on that line and change leads, this time from the right lead back to the left. I hold my horse steady with my hands, shift my weight from the left hip to the right and now press with my right leg to move his hips to the left so he can change leads. Next, I again lope my horse on that straight line for a hundred yards or so before gradually bending him into a left-hand circle.

If your horse has successfully changed leads both ways the first time you ask him to, then that is plenty for that day. If he doesn't change leads and gets a little excited or anything like that, then you need to reassure him and go back to work on moving his hips.

Caution: Don't get into a battle with this horse and say, "I'm going to make you change leads today." That's not the approach to take. If you try a lead change each way and he's

not successful, then leave it until tomorrow. Start where you left off and continue to work on the change in the same way. Keep working with this program until your horse is comfortable changing leads in this manner—from a circle to a straight line, then gradually bending back into the other circle.

A Quiet Change

There a few more things that you should do if you are going to preserve this horse and make him a quiet lead-changer all the time for years to come.

For example, I lope my horse in five, six, seven left-hand circles at a medium speed; then I change my horse's lead to the right but continue loping in the left-hand circle. My horse has been in the left lead, has changed

Counter-cantering, for example, on the left lead while in a right-hand circle can be a powerful tool to help keep your horse listening to you and changing leads quietly without anticipating the change.

ROSS HECOX

to the right lead, but now is counter-cantering in a left-hand circle. He struggles with this for a little bit because counter-cantering is uncomfortable for him. So I lope him in this left circle on his right lead a couple of times, and then break to a trot or change him back to the left lead and lope another half-circle.

Remember: You want to let the horse know that a change in lead is not a change in direction. This exercise enforces that idea.

Then, of course, you do the same things to counter-canter your horse in the other direction. Lope him in the right lead on a right-hand circle; then change to lope on the left lead so that your horse again counter-canters.

Another thing I do when changing leads and using a counter-canter is somewhat the opposite. This time, I lope a left circle quietly with my horse in the left lead and come across the middle in the arena. Next, I just guide him into the right-hand circle but don't let my horse change leads. This makes him go from the correct lead on the left circle into a counter-canter on the right circle.

I stay on the left lead in the right circle — and circle and circle. Then as I'm going around one time and go past the center of the arena, I ride along the side wall, where I change leads and my horse goes into the correct lead. All this helps make sure that my horse doesn't relate changing a lead with changing his direction.

There's one other thing I do to avoid my horse anticipating. In practice I almost never make a lead change in the center of the pen.

Two important points: You always make your lead changes from a position of collection and always when traveling in a straight line. Say you are going around in a circle — especially a fast circle — and your horse is shaped to that circle. All of a sudden you stick your outside leg away from the horse, straighten him and kick him into a fast lead change going the other way. That can give your horse some anxiety. Doing that teaches him to get excited and worried, and to rush into lead changes.

You don't ever want a horse to worry about a lead change because, as you know, that horse is a prey animal and his way of dealing with fear or a threatening situation is to run. You don't want the horse to come across the middle, change leads and then take off because he is scared of what might happen.

Everything has to be quiet, collected, and soft. You must think through your lead changes very well and make sure that you're not scaring your horse. If you work on lead changes for a couple of days and you see that your horse is showing apprehension, just leave lead changes alone for a day or two. Do other things and then come back to the lead changes.

Once I have a horse changing leads softly without speeding up or showing any apprehension or stress, I might change him twice a week and occasionally three times a week. I don't make a big deal about lead changes, just change often enough that the horse knows what I'm asking him to do. This way, he's not scared of a lead change and not wondering about it, and he doesn't at any time associate a lead change with a change of direction.

In Summary

- Circling is the first step in the horse's advanced education. There are three parts to teaching a horse to circle—his position in the circle, the redirection and speed control.

- The horse learns to maintain and be responsible for his circle position, keeping his body arced along the circle he's traveling, and for maintaining that frame on his own as he travels.

- Redirection is the ability to guide and redirect the horse with the outside or inside rein. The horse should rein into or out of the circle equally well.

- The rider's body position controls the horse's speed in the circles.

- The canter departure combines basic number two and basic number three to have the horse move from a standstill into a collected lope.

- The timing of a lead change is as critical as the method used to ask the horse to change leads.

- When teaching a horse to change leads, it's very important that the horse never relate the change in lead to a change of direction.

13

Stops and Rollbacks

Before moving ahead to have advanced conversations with your horse about stops and rollbacks, it's really important that you and your horse communicate well and consistently, using the three basics previously discussed. First, your horse should be flexible from side to side, soft and giving. Next, when you gather the slack in your reins, your horse should be soft in the poll as you squeeze him forward with both legs. Finally, you should be able to move your horse's hips to the right and to the left.

Using these three basics routinely keeps the lines of communication open with your horse. Make these basics part of your warm-up routine and your day's ride, no matter what you plan to do with your horse. Mastering these basics signals that your horse is ready to progress to advanced maneuvers.

The Stop Position

If you watch from the side and a horse is loping in the left lead, for example, you notice that as his front end travels down toward the ground and then up, the horse pushes off from behind. The front end is in air and then both front feet land. Both hind feet are being pulled up underneath him. Then his hind feet come down, and he pushes with both hind feet;

the front end again comes up, extends and reaches forward to hit the ground. The process just keeps repeating itself.

If you examine this a little closer, you find out if this horse is loping with a three-beat gait. In other words, his leading front leg, when he's in the left lead, is his left front leg. When that leg goes to the ground on the first beat, at that point his front end is down and all three other legs are off the ground. The right front is in the air and both hind feet are being carried forward underneath the horse's body. As the hind feet go to the ground and the horse prepares to push forward, the horse's front end comes up and, again, the whole process is repeated.

When that leading leg is on the ground, that's beat one. In the next step of the sequence, the leading leg comes off the ground, and his left hind and right front go to the ground at the same time; that's beat two. The third beat occurs when that right hind foot hits the ground.

As the horse's leading left front is on the ground and both hind feet are moving underneath him, if he decides to stop at that point in his stride, all he has to do is drop his rear end. His shoulders are up right then and his head and neck are relaxed. The

The best way I can encourage my horse to make consistently smooth stops is to make sure the three basics are part of his daily warm-up routine.

horse is in perfect stop position. With the hind feet under the horse, all he has to do is relax and quit moving to be perfectly positioned to stop.

At any other point in that horse's stride, he's not going to be able to stop easily and smoothly like he can in that perfect stop position. If you try to make the horse stop, for example, when both hind feet are on the ground and he's pushing with them, then all you can do is pull his head back and up into the air, causing him to hit with all four feet on the ground. Then he has to gather himself again and make another big lunge before he is able to be in that good stopping position.

So, if you want a pretty stop from that horse, the message to stop must get to your horse's brain as his leading front leg is on the ground and both hind feet are coming beneath him.

"Whoa" is Key

How does a rider achieve that? How does any rider time his stop cue perfectly to put the horse in the most effective position to stop well?

I don't think that anyone in the world has the timing to send a horse down the track, as fast as the horse can run, and say to himself, "Okay, his leading leg is going on the ground now, so if I pull at this exact moment, it's a good time to stop." No one has that kind of timing.

So, instead, what I have to do is teach my horse that when I say the word "whoa," no matter at what point in his stride the horse happens to be, he can go ahead and finish that stride. When he does, the leading leg is on the ground, his hind legs are underneath him, and at that point his rear end drops to be in stop position. I want my horse to be

The easiest point in the stride to ask a horse to drop the hindquarters into a smooth stop is when the leading foreleg is on the ground and the hind feet are moving forward to come underneath the horse's body.

ROSS HECOX

150

confident that when he hears the word whoa, that means I always give him time to get into position and execute the stop.

So how do I go about this? The way I'm going to teach here in the book is an unorthodox way. A lot of people might disagree with this, but it is a system that I have used and taught to a lot of people. It's worked for me and it has worked for them, and I'm sure it can work for anyone.

First, understand that if I decide to teach a horse to stop as his leading leg goes to the ground, say whoa, and pull on the horse with both reins, essentially I would be teaching that horse to push. Probably 75 percent of the colts I have ridden have learned that whoa means their riders are going to pull first—before the young horses have even learned that whoa means to stop. As a result, when a colt handled that way hears that word, he wants to push. When he does, he pushes his center of gravity onto his front end—and that spoils the stop before the colt ever gets to it.

What I use is a system in which I stop a horse with one rein. Then, the horse is not going to be able to push against that one rein, he is going to be light in the stop, and he goes to the ground softly and with a lot more lightness than he would otherwise.

Why Whoa?

Sometimes people wonder why it is so important to teach a horse to stop on whoa. At the beginning stage of stopping, the horse knows nothing about that word—whoa. So, I lope a horse in a circle and say whoa. I might as well have said, "What did you have for breakfast?" or "Did you have a good dinner last night?" It doesn't make any difference because this horse isn't going to acknowledge anything that I might stay.

But, when I say whoa, I wait just a second—actually quite a bit less than a second—but there is a little bit of a pause there. Next, I use the inside rein just to balance the horse and keep him from turning his head and neck. I primarily use the outside rein to pull the horse to a stop and then pull him around to go the other way.

In the beginning this isn't a pretty sight. The horse doesn't know what's happening. He probably hits on all fours first, then goes crooked and swings his rear end around toward his front. That's okay. I then just use my legs to urge him into a lope going in the other direction.

I lope the horse around a little bit, two or three circles, and let him relax again. Then I say whoa again—and nothing happens. The horse doesn't acknowledge whoa because he doesn't know what I'm talking about. So as I say whoa again, wait just a millisecond, and then take hold of my outside rein again. I pull the horse to a stop, then pull him around to the side and kick him up in a lope the other way. Again—not a pretty sight. I keep doing these same things until I've done them 10 or 12 times in the course of the first day. And, of course, I do the same things again the second day.

If this is a smart colt at all, he figures out pretty quickly that whoa means he should prepare himself. He starts being aware that when he hears whoa, his rider is going to pull him around to the side and kick him forward in the other direction. Soon the horse is going to make things as easy as possible on himself and starts to prepare for the stop by getting his rear in the ground, keeping his shoulders up. Then, when I pull the horse around, all he has to do is push with his hind foot, and he's right back into his lope going the other way—and it is easy.

This horse is going to respond that way eventually. At some point, the minute that I say whoa and he starts to use his rear end, instead of pulling him around, I stop right then. I rub his neck and pet him a little bit. I want to let him know that he did a good job. Then I walk the horse around a little circle, lope him the other way and then do the same things again.

Whenever the horse makes an effort to stop and roll back, to turn to go the other way, I give him a reward. I pet him to reinforce that he did the right thing. My hands are going to be a lot softer on his mouth or his nose, depending on whether I have a hackamore or a snaffle bit on the horse. I'm much kinder with my hands when he makes an effort than I am when he doesn't make an effort. I'm not going to be harsh and I don't jerk, but I do use a little more force and pressure with my hands when the horse doesn't respond. When he does respond, I use little pressure with my hands. Everything that I do tells this horse, " Yes. When you stop, you're doing the right thing."

If I continue to do these things and this horse has any athletic ability at all, within three or four days every time I say whoa, he's starting to go to the ground. He begins to do

Early in training, the word "whoa" usually doesn't mean much to a horse, so I help him to understand that ignoring or resisting whoa isn't the desired response.
ROSS HECOX

The horse needs to understand and stop on whoa in a collected "ready" position—ready to do something more, maybe back up or turn and go the other way.
ROSS HECOX

To encourage the horse's understanding, when I sense resistance to the whoa cue and stop, I immediately pull the horse to a stop and turn him around to go in the other direction.
ROSS HECOX

Then I immediately drive the horse forward and ask for a lope. Soon the horse understands that when I say whoa, he can push the "easy" button by making a nice collected stop.
ROSS HECOX

that with more and more authority because he is in a hurry to get to the little rest period, get rubbed and petted a little bit and stand there.

So from this point, that's my approach to stopping the horse. I lope him in a circle and say whoa. When he goes to the ground with some authority, I let him stand there. When he gives it a half-hearted effort, I pull him around and kick him up to lope the other way. If he doesn't give that much of an effort, I also ask him to increase his speed a little bit. In other words, after I've pulled him around and asked for the lope, I might run him faster around the circle a couple of times to really make him work. Whenever the horse does a good job and hits that stop, I let him stand and rub him a little. When I do pull to send him the other way, I don't want to expend much effort and I want a nice and gentle lope—and I'm going to be just as nice to him as I can.

Understanding how the hands work at this point is important. When I turn the horse with the direct rein, in this case the outside rein, I balance him with the other rein so that I don't pull his head around until I am actually ready for him to roll back the other way. When I am ready for him to turn back, I give a big release with the inside rein and the outside rein pulls his nose all the way across and through the turn. It is very important to be able to do this especially well with any colt and I must have very well-developed basics— numbers one, two and three—in order to do these things successfully.

Straight Lines

Within a couple of weeks, three at the very most, the horse is stopping consistently on the circle. It should take just a pickup of the outside rein to make him fold right over his hock and roll back to go the other direction.

As soon as he does this consistently on the circles, I stop circling and start stopping that horse on straight lines. Otherwise, I do the exact same things to stop. I lope the horse straight, say whoa, and then wait for him to initiate the stop. I use my hands just to balance him after he initiates the stop on his own and hold him in the ground just until the forward motion stops.

When I lope a horse at this stage, I never know whether I'm going to pull him around and send him back the other way, or if I'm going to stop and let him stand there. That's totally up to the horse. If his mind is wandering a little bit when he lopes and I say whoa,

When a green horse travels and stops straight, everything's fine, and he gets to relax and stand. Otherwise, he goes back to work, turning and loping again.

ROSS HECOX

he might give a half-hearted effort, so I pull him and kick him to send him the other direction. If I say whoa and he breaks in his back to get into the ground and really tries to stop,

I let him stand. The horse is always the one who dictates what happens after I say whoa. When I stay with the program, a colt can become very consistent very quickly, and this works just as well on an old horse as it does on a young horse.

When you lope or gallop a horse and say whoa, if he bounces and pushes with his nose and does all those things you don't want a

If a horse doesn't travel straight, the stop can't be straight and smooth. At this point, the important thing is to correct his path of travel first, using my legs and, if necessary, my hands.

ROSS HECOX

horse to do, there's only one thing to do. You must pull him around and kick him into a lope the other way.

An old horse that has been taught to stop properly, by whatever method at one time or another, figures this out quickly. I can say whoa and pull him around a few times, and he starts going to the ground in a hurry. In the past I've been asked to ride a lot of old horses that had quit stopping for somebody and after about five minutes on the track they have been stopping very well. This is not an exercise that's just limited to young horses. It's an exercise that can be used on any horse of any age.

Straight to the Stop

Having a horse that can run straight is an important element in stopping smoothly. If your horse doesn't run straight, he can't stop. He starts to stop, but one foot stays in the ground and the other one comes out several times, or your horse leans one way or the other and doesn't want to start running straight when you ask him.

You want him to stay there on that line, without trying to lean on way or the other. Do the following to get that horse traveling in a straight line.

For example, you're loping your horse in a left lead, trying to gallop a straight line across a pasture or wherever you might be. Your horse starts to fade to the right. The first thing you need to do is tap, tap, tap him with your right leg; try to move the horse back over to the line, where you want him to be. When you tap with your leg and he moves toward the line, that's fine.

If you tap several times with your leg and he doesn't move onto that line and start running straight, you must put him back on the line—and immediately drop your hands when you do. If the horse starts fading to the right again, you tap, tap, tap and then forcibly use the reins to move him back onto this line. Keep repeating this correction until you can gallop your horse and he runs a straight line. After you have done this for a while, your horse should run on a straight line anywhere you put him, as long as you don't run and stop him again and again on that same line.

You want your horse to run straight, but when schooling him on straight lines, you don't want to spur him to go faster; you don't want to knock around on him until he's scared. You only want him to travel on that straight line and stay on that line. No matter if he fades left or right, or which lead he is using, he must go straight or you're not going to have a good stop.

Whether you are going down the fence or up and down the middle of an arena, it is essential that you school your horse on running straight, as well as accelerating and decelerating. A horse doesn't stop well unless he is accelerating as he runs forward. Think about this: If you are in a boat and the motor is in the back, that's where the driving force comes from. In a horse, the driving force is in his hind legs and he must drive forward to stop.

Speed

So at this point your horse is stopping on whoa. He's light, has his shoulders up and goes to the ground with authority from a slow easy lope. Now it is time to step up the program just a little bit.

Start running your horse a little faster than that slow lope. As you send him forward with a little more speed and authority, and say whoa, he's going to try to give the same response. But because he's moving faster than he has been, that upsets his timing a little bit.

Make allowances for this and give the horse a day or two to get comfortable with the fast timing. If he continues to have trouble with the speed and timing, drop back to the previous level at which you had been riding. Regain the horse's confidence, then try the fast speed again, and he probably can handle it very well.

It is important in all these exercises that you never overload the horse's capabilities. You don't want him to get worried or scared of stopping. You want everything your horse must do to become part of his everyday routine— something you expect him to do, just like he expects you to feed him and clean his stall.

When your horse handles the additional speed well and is very consistent, stay at the same speed for a while. When he becomes very comfortable with that speed, move the speed up another notch. If you do this during a course of a couple months, you can have a horse that is very consistent at every speed.

Dealing With Dirt

When my horse is stopping well, I stop him only once or twice every day, simply because this is a skill that requires timing,

As with any maneuver, once a horse is comfortable stopping at a lope, it's time to pick up speed. The increased speed might throw off the horse's timing, but I can always slow down and let him regain his confidence in making that stop.

ROSS HECOX

balance, and responsiveness. If I don't stop a horse on a frequent basis, he gets rusty and doesn't stop as well or as consistently as he has been.

However, I seldom run a horse wide open and then stop him. I stop him from a slow lope or at medium speed, and on any kind of ground. I just want that horse to lope down the track. When I say whoa, I want to get a confident response from a horse, to know that he is able to finish the stride that he's in and, once that is done, complete the stop.

I also want my horse to stop on any kind of pull. Here's what I mean: If I go to arena somewhere and the ground is really good, I want to be able to send the horse down the pen with some speed and authority before I say whoa. Just as I feel his body go to the ground, I want to drop my hand and let that slack just hang there; I let the horse finish the stop all the way to the end on that loose rein.

Sometimes I take the horse to an arena where the ground is more difficult, requiring more push so the horse has to put forth a lot of effort to hold the stop. In this situation, I lope the horse, say whoa, then take a hold of him with light pressure. I hold onto his face throughout that stop, right to the end, without any head-shaking or resistance from the horse at all.

When the ground is like a plowed field with a lot of dampness to it, that, too, requires a great deal of push from the horse. In this case, I again send that horse with the same speed and say whoa. As I pull the slack out of the reins, I want the horse to gather that ground with the same amount of authority and let me pull on him as hard as necessary to keep him in the ground until the end of the stop.

The Rollback

At this point, I have talked a lot about stops, but not much about rollbacks. In the beginning a colt soon learns one thing if he doesn't go to the ground with some authority when he hears the word whoa, and I ask him to stop. He learns that at the end of the stop, I can pull him around and send him in the other direction. He's also learned that the best way to handle that possibility is to get in that ground deeply and hold the stop. By now the horse keeps his shoulders up and is able to tip his nose, bend his neck and flow right across one hock and leave, going back along that same set of tracks that he made coming

into the stop. That's actually what I want in an ideal rollback.

However, there is more I need to do to perfect and define the rollback. When I have the colt stopping really well and consistently, it's time to make a differentiation between my stop and a rollback. If I don't do this, the colt is going to get the idea that he runs down there, hits that stop and goes one way or the other. I don't always want that response. Instead, I want the horse to have the willingness to run and hit that stop all the way to the end—and then wait for me to tell him whether he's going to roll back or not.

To do this, develop that "wait," I have to mix up things a bit. When the horse is stopping really well and I don't have to worry about a lot of inconsistencies, I just send him straight and stop him straight, and then let him stand there. I might let him stand there a minute or two. Then I lay the rein against his neck and ask him to roll right back over the tracks. he just made

In the beginning that waiting period, before he turns back, is going to be a surprise to the horse. Then I drag the reins across his neck and enforce this rollback with the direct rein, pull him back over his hocks and send him out the other way with my leg. As I continue to do this exercise, the horse becomes better performing it.

Sometimes I stop the horse, let him stand a second or two, and then roll him back. Sometimes I stop him, let him stand for two minutes and then ask for the rollback. Sometimes I stop him, let him stand a few minutes and then back him. Or I stop him, let him stand for a minute or two, and then walk the horse forward.

I never want to do anything that this horse is going to find predictable, so that he starts to know what I'm going to do next. Preventing that anticipation is something I must carry out through the stop and rollback training program so that the horse can have a clean, straight, forward stop and doesn't lean one way or the other.

An important note at this point: When I roll the horse back to my left, I always use my left hand with four fingers between the reins. I drag the slack from the outside rein across the horse's neck and enforce the command with the direct rein. When I roll the horse back to the right, I change hands. With reins in my right hand I drag the slack of the left rein across his neck and enforce the

To perfect the rollback, the horse must learn to wait for my direction and I must add finesse to maneuvers the horse already understands, such as the rundown to the rollback.
DARRELL DODDS

This is the sweet spot, that moment of suspension when I can ask the horse to stop and he's in position to perform the maneuver easily and well.
DARRELL DODDS

command with my right rein and, of course, with my outside leg. I give the horse the same cue from either side and from the same spot so there's no change. It is very important that I keep the cues exactly the same, equal on both sides of the horse's neck and mouth, in order to have a horse that is completely equal on both sides.

The point comes when I do put one finger between the reins and use one hand. But the cue is still in the same spot, place, and direction. It doesn't matter if I'm riding a 3-, 4-, 6- or 10-year-old; most of the time, when I roll a horse back, I have four fingers in the reins exactly as I have described. Occasionally I put one finger between the reins to check out a horse, to make sure everything is working as well as possibly can be. Then I go back to the four fingers just to keep everything easy and honest.

Once stopped, the horse's understanding of "wait" is critical at this point. He must wait for me to tell him if we're just stopping or stopping and turning.
DARRELL DODDS

When a horse understands how to stop in a collected manner, in that "ready" stance, it's easy to redirect him to go the other way.
DARRELL DODDS

Stopping a horse or rolling him back is very systematic, an orchestrated procedure of making what I want the horse to do easy and what I don't want the horse to do difficult. I use the horse's natural tendency to make things easy on himself. This way I am able to get a horse to stop and do a rollback with great degree of difficulty, yet the horse stays equal. In other words, he performs a rollback well to either side, in either direction.

Because the horse is ready for the next maneuver, the rollback, he never loses his momentum, which helps carry him through the turn.
DARRELL DODDS

With the turn complete, it's also easy to direct and drive the horse forward out of the rollback, thanks to previous work on the three basics.
DARRELL DODDS

Straightness is important when leaving one rollback to go to another rollback, just as straightness is when stopping, backing or changing leads
DARRELL DODDS

"At this time in a horse's development you should notice an interesting phenomenon ...he automatically starts to step into the turnaround."

14

Spins

In this chapter you are going to learn about teaching the horse to spin or turn around. Many people think that when you teach a horse to spin, the first thing you do is rock back on the horse to get him on his inside hind pivot foot. Then you try to teach the front end to walk around the pivot foot.

In my opinion this is the furthest thing from the truth. What I want instead is for my horse to be very forward. I want to be thinking forward and I want my horse thinking forward movement all the time, and I want him moving in a forward direction as I start to teach him to turn around.

Walk the Circle

I begin by having my horse walk about a 15-foot circle. I walk this circle until I have control on this horse. I don't want to have to pull him back into the circle or for the horse to ride out of the circle. I just want to walk this little circle and use my inside rein to tip my horse's nose into the circle a little bit. Once in a while, I use my inside leg to push him out of the circle or use my outside leg to push him back into the circle. I want this horse to walk that 15-foot circle almost like he is on autopilot.

Once I achieve that, I start to draw down this 15-foot circle a little smaller and smaller until the horse is almost walking his front end around his rear end. I want the rear end to be almost stationary as he uses his front end to walk around his hindquarters. This can be a little awkward for the horse. He's going to be using that inside front leg to stride forward all the time. As I ask him to make the circle smaller and smaller, he's probably thinking that this idea isn't working very well but he's still trying to do it.

At the very minute the horse quits taking that forward stride with his inside front leg and takes a little bit of a lateral step, I drop the reins and ask him to move forward out of the circle and let him relax. From the very first time I ask a horse to move out of this little circle, I lean forward, run my hand out and over his neck with four fingers between the reins, use my outside leg to step the horse forward and drive him out of the circle.

Handling the Reins

It is extremely important that when I go to the left, I have four fingers in between the reins, which are crossed, and use my left hand. When I go to

To develop a spin, you must maintain the drive and impulsion for forward movement and simply redirect that energy to one side or the other.

DARRELL DODDS

Walking a 15-foot circle so consistently that the horse seems to be on autopilot lays the foundation for a horse to perform spins well.

ROSS HECOX

By gradually reducing the diameter of the 15-foot circle, the horse is almost walking the forehand around the hindquarters.

ROSS HECOX

the right, I'm going to have four fingers in between the reins and I'm going to use my right hand. If I want a horse to turn around the same way consistently, I need to be able to use each hand effectively.

I manipulate those reins in order to help this horse understand what I want him to do. For the turn, at first, I set my inside rein, the direct rein, maybe 3 to 4 inches shorter than my outside, indirect rein. When I use this rein to draw the circle down a little smaller or to tip the horse's nose to the inside a little bit, I lightly draw the slack. I want to be able

to rub the outside rein across the outside of this horse's neck—just before I make contact with the corner of his mouth with the inside rein.

I use my elbow a lot and keep my forearm and wrist straight. I want to keep a straight line from the rein to my wrist and my elbow when I make contact with this horse's mouth. My elbow is able to come all the way back to my hipbone, and I should be able to take my hand back as far as I need in order to get this horse to respond. That's the same for turning to either side.

When crossing your reins and using them with one hand, you basically want to create a straight line from the rein to your wrist and your elbow.
ROSS HECOX

As the walking circle becomes small and tight, your horse can take that first small lateral step, as shown here, to the right, and you then immediately release him to walk forward.
ROSS HECOX

Convey the Signals

In a left-hand turn my weight is going to be on my outside or right hipbone, my right leg close to the horse's body, my left leg out and away from the horse's body. Remember: This is when turning the horse to the left. Every part of my body is giving a signal, conveying to this horse that we are going to the left.

So I'm walking this circle to the left and I'm sitting on my right hip. My right leg is close to the horse's ribcage, my left leg out and away from his side. I draw the slack from the rein and draw the circle down a little smaller and smaller until the horse's rear end practically walks around his front end. Then the horse takes that first lateral step with his left front. I lean forward and run my hand up his neck, and with my outside leg ride this horse forward again, straight out of the circle. I drop my hands, relax, and pet him a little bit. Then I turn the horse in the same direction as before and walk the circle in the same direction, and try to do the exact same things again.

Hopefully, the second time I give these signals, that little lateral step comes quicker than it did the first time. Maybe the third time the little lateral step comes even faster. I do seven, eight, or nine walks to the left, going around the circle, getting that lateral

step and walking the horse out of the circle. I let the horse relax a little bit and then go to the right.

The reason I do things this way is that a horse does not associate what he has been asked to do to the left with doing that same thing to the right. He learns faster by doing several repetitions to the left, and then working to the right, rather than going left, right, left, right and so forth. So it is very important that with any exercise I do it several times to the left and then change to the right.

The Second Step

I've been working at this circle for several weeks now. Every time I ask my horse to go to the left, walk the circle and draw it down, he's to the point that his rear end is about to stop and his front end keeps on going. The

horse takes that lateral step and then I push him forward out of the circle. When the horse becomes so consistent that every single time I ride the circle down and he takes one step to the side, I ask him to take two lateral steps. After the first little step, instead of leaning forward and running my hand over his neck and using my outside leg to ride him forward, I wait for a second step. One, two steps and then I lean forward, move my hand above his neck, use my outside leg and ride him forward from the circle.

I do these same things until the horse consistently takes two lateral steps every time. Then I move up to three steps. Once he is consistent with three lateral steps, I ask him for four. Four steps is a complete 360-degree turn.

Now that I have accomplished all that, I can walk my horse in a circle, lead his nose

As your horse's understanding grows, so does his confidence in making that lateral step a big one. Then it's time to ask for more.

ROSS HECOX

Ultimately, your horse figures out the next natural progression following that big lateral step—crossing the outside foreleg over the inside one.

ROSS HECOX

into the turn, do a 360-degree turn and walk back into my circle again. Then I walk two or three times around that circle and again lead my horse's nose into that turn; one, two, three, four steps to make a 360-degree turn; and walk back onto my circle again.

I do that whole exercise for a while. The thing about the turnaround is that I develop it in very small increments, and I don't want to get in a hurry. I want a colt or any horse to do things at his own pace and be consistent in anything that he learns. I don't want that horse to be worried about anything.

The Second 360

When a horse 100-percent consistently walks this circle and steps into this baby 360-degree turnaround, then steps right back into the circle, I move him up to two 360-degree turns. Later I can add more.

At the stage of two steps, three steps, four steps, or even one-and-a-half turns, if that horse makes a little mistake—leaning to the inside, hurrying to the outside or inside, wanting to jump out of the turn, or showing any inconsistency—I simply push him forward out of the turnaround. I want this firmly planted in the horse's mind: If he makes a little mistake or has a problem while he's turning, the way to get out of the problem is to go forward. That is a very important lesson for any horse to learn.

Speed Management

When the horse consistently can do two 360-degree turns well every time, he's ready to pick up speed. Speeding up a horse is a delicate stage because you don't want your horse to get worried about turning around; increasing the speed, even a little, can affect his timing. Never ever ask your horse to speed up with your hand. The only actions your hands make are to rub the slack of the outside rein across your horse's neck and to lead with the inside rein.

All the impulsion to increase the horse's speed has to come from your leg. Use your outside leg a little stronger than you have been and with a little bumping motion. Before, all you did was press on the horse's side. Now you start by pressing until the horse gets going and then you bump, bump till he speeds up a little bit, and then you move him out in a walk. You then turn him around the same way and again bump to speed him up through the turn before you move the horse

The more consistently you work on the spin basics at a slow rate of speed, the more efficiently your horse performs, and speed comes as a natural result of developing that efficient movement.
ROSS HECOX

out of the circle. You also must do those same things in the other direction.

Ask for speed only in very small increments. Soon your horse turns around twice very consistently, very smoothly, does a good job and tries really hard for you. He hardly ever makes a mistake, so you can ask him for a little more speed—bump, bump, bump—and you just keep doing this.

It is very important that you don't forget about your slow speeds. You always want your horse or colt to start slowly and build speed, and then step out of the turn. You still are doing the same things—walking the circle, drawing it down, turning this horse around. You're just doing these same things a little faster, cleaner, and snappier than before.

If your horse starts to get a little tangled up or seems like he's getting confused, maybe bumping his knee or stepping on a hoof, you are going to slow him down. You help him rebuild some confidence before you speed him up again. To do that, be very consistent in the way you use your hands and legs; do not change the program on your horse a single bit.

So now you have this horse that that can turn around two, three, four, five or six times, and he's getting faster, hardly ever making any mistakes. At this stage, the more you turn him around, the more your horse starts to speed up on his own.

This just comes from efficiency. The better your horse handles the turnaround, the more he speeds up on his own. If he's a lazy colt, you might want to bump him a little stronger with that outside leg, but this is a judgment call you, as the rider, make. If your horse turns around really well with a decent amount of speed and as many times as you want, doesn't suck back over his hocks, doesn't want to step forward out of the turn and just keeps turning until you extend your hand and lean forward to ride him out of the turn, you're in an ideal position.

As time goes on, you can let your horse build a little more speed but you don't ever want to forget about working at the slower speeds. It's important, as you turn, to be able to vary your horse's speed by the way you use your leg. Whether you are in a show pen or riding a horse or colt at home, you want him to start into the turn softly and quietly. Once you feel that he has the cadence, you ask him for a little more speed or you just keep him at that low speed. Always remember that your hand is the steering wheel and you leg is the accelerator.

Add Finesse

When your horse turns around really well and rapidly, and has a lot of confidence, the next step is to quit walking those little circles prior to turning him around. Stop your horse and let him stand there a minute. Then rock him forward or step him forward a little and turn him around a couple of times; then push him forward out of the turnaround. Keep doing these things but always make sure your horse is working at the speed you want and that everything is the way you want it to be.

At this time in a horse's development, you should notice an interesting phenomenon. As you rub the indirect rein slack across your horse's neck and pick up the direct rein with your hand, before the direct rein ever gets to the corner of the horse's mouth, he automatically starts to step into the turnaround. When this starts happening on a consistent basis,

Although one finger between the reins is typical in competition, the best way to ensure quality in your horse's performance is to work at home as usual with the reins crossed in one hand.

ROSS HECOX

To develop a light response, allow your horse time enough to learn to initiate the turnaround when the slack outside, indirect rein—not a tight one—rubs against his neck.
DARRELL DODDS

Always be sure those initial steps in performing multiple spins are correct before you ask your horse for any speed.
DARRELL DODDS

Establishing correctness first reinforces the efficiency of movement that's necessary to build speed in the spin or any maneuver.
DARRELL DODDS

your horse is responding to the preparatory command of the slack of the rein against his neck before the direct rein ever comes into play. As he gets better at the turnaround, the horse starts to rely totally on that outside rein as the cause for initiating the turnaround.

The only time that inside, direct rein comes into play is when the horse is slow starting, is distracted and doesn't start at all, or if he doesn't step into the turnaround as alertly as you think he should. Then with a sharp bump to that inside rein, you say, "Let's go!"

At this point you begin to employ this indirect-rein method of initiating the turnaround more and the direct-rein method less.

You still use four fingers in between the reins, and everything else is the same except that you start to rely more and more on the neck-rein. When your horse gets pretty good at that, you put only one finger between the reins and use your riding hand to do the exact same things, make the same motions, that you've been doing with four fingers between the reins.

Throughout the transition to the indirect neck-rein, never let the outside rein get tight. That's an absolute no-no. Your horse has to learn to step into the turnaround and turn off the slack of the outside rein. Experiment with this once a week, but remember that most

always you have four fingers in between the reins. How many fingers you have there just depends on your horse's progress but take your time making this transition from four fingers to one during the turnaround. Later, when you get to a horse show, work your horse both ways—with four fingers in the reins and then with one finger between them. Then, take your horse him into the arena and show him.

From this point, your horse is pretty much trained to turn around. If you follow the guidelines for a period of time, your horse continues to improve. As his footwork becomes more familiar, he gets better at his job.

Remember to keep doing the exact same things with your horse and remain very consistent. The mistake many people make: A person gets a horse to the point he turns around while the rider uses one hand and has only one finger in between the reins—then the rider turns the horse that way all the time. In that situation the horse's performance can't help but deteriorate. It is very important to turn your horse around with four fingers in the reins in the training scenario, the biggest part of the time you're riding at home. Do things the same way at the show. By doing so, your horse always is there for you and he's always consistent.

Profile
Dick Pieper

Richard Dale Pieper was born in 1939 on a farm near Portsmouth in southern Ohio. His parents, Dale and Ruth Peiper, ran a farm that raised cattle, sheep and horses in the foothills of the Appalachian Mountains. From childhood, Dick rode a horse—gathering livestock or just roaming.

When Dick was 13, his father's outside job necessitated that he travel four days a week. At that point, the Piepers had more than 300 head of sheep and cattle, and the horses. Unable to find reliable help, Dale told his son that if they were going to keep the farm, Dick would have to take over. His father would pay Dick $15 a week. Dick remembers, "I was floored by the fact he'd pay me that much and flattered by the responsibility."

Every morning Dick rose early, saddled a horse and rode the mile to the farm to feed, checked for calves and lambs, then he rode back and fed all the horses. He'd take a quick shower and catch the school bus. He did the same thing every evening and when it was time for heifers to calve or ewes to lamb, he stayed in the barn in a little room with a propane heater. There was a bench and a desk, and Dick did his homework and watched the livestock. It was a seven-day-a-week job but he enjoyed what he was doing, and the work ethic it instilled would last a lifetime.

Dale and Ruth wanted their son to be a veterinarian but Dick really, really wanted to be a horse trainer. In deference to his parents, he began working his way through school at Ohio State, but the draft and the specter of Viet Nam were looming, so he enlisted in the then U.S. Naval Reserve. At the end of his inactive duty, he went into the Navy for two years. He had married prior to leaving and his son, Brad, was born while Dick was away.

Out of the Navy, and in spite of the failure of his marriage, Dick was ready to live his dream. He returned to the family place, built 16 stalls and began to train—everything. At that time few trainers specialized, so he showed in halter, pleasure, trail, reining, roping—pretty much every event the American Quarter Horse Association offered. He liked the reining and cutting best, but had to take a variety of horses just to make a living.

Before long Dick's success had been noticed. He moved just outside of Pittsburg, working for E.T. Halo. Halo owned a construction business and his facility boasted a nice indoor arena, paved driveways and beautiful stalls—plus the chance to ride good horses. By then beginning to specialize in reining, Dick received his first national recognition, showing one of Halo's horses, Mr. Jim 45, to the title of American Quarter Horse Association 1972 Honor Roll Reining Stallion.

The National Reining Horse Association was in its infancy and the first futurity had been held in 1966. It was when he joined the NRHA that Dick began to build the record that would lead a lifetime of accomplishment and a Hall of Fame induction. His first NRHA earnings came in 1974 and he qualified for the prestigious NRHA Futurity Finals in 1976 when he finished third on Donnada Cody, owned by Jay Capone from Miami, Florida.

By then Dick's reining career was flourishing. He won the 1977 NRHA Futurity on the gelding, Spanish Mountain, owned by Bill and Pauline Haggis from Connecticut. Dick was co-reserve champion of the 1979 Futurity on the good mare Cee Blair Masota, owned by Crawford Williams of Raleigh, N.C., and rode her to his first American Quarter Horse Association world championship in junior reining.

In 1980, Dick had two top-ten finalists at the NRHA Futurity—and one of them, finishing fifth, was a talented full sister to Cee Blair Masota named Miss Cee Blair, owned by Rae B. Williams.

In 1984, after a six-year stint in North Carolina, Dick then was offered a job by

Dick Herr, manager of the horse division of Willowbrook Farm in Catasaqua, Pennsylvania. Willowbrook, located just south of Allentown, was broadly known as the best reining horse breeding facility in the world. At the time there were only two farms selectively breeding for reiners—Willowbrook and the Bob Loomis Ranch.

Dick showed Miss Cee Blair to win the title of 1985 NRHA Open World Champion, setting a record for money earned that was not broken until 1994 when her Topsail Cody son, Cee Blair Sailor, shattered that record.

Also very active in the governance of the NRHA, Dick served as the association's president for five years in the late 1980s. During his tenure as president, innovations were made that would change the entire industry. He remembers, "A lot of people were talking about how difficult it was to judge so many horses in the futurity and keep it all straight. There was a lot of buzz about it."

At the 1983 NRHA Futurity, legendary reiner and first-ever Million Dollar Rider Bill Horn had an exciting run in the finals on a horse called Enterprise Velvet. Craig Johnson, another future Million Dollar Rider, had a very correct run with no penalties on Lucky Bay Glo. The judges named Craig the winner. It was a visible forum for arguments both against and for a new judging system. Some said the correctness should have won; others said that although Horn trotted out of a rollback, there was actually no penalty for that at the time, and the more dynamic maneuvers should have taken the title.

Dick continues, "Ben Mears owned Enterprise Velvet and after the futurity was completed, he sued the NRHA because his horse didn't win. By his own admission it was a frivolous lawsuit but he knew the NRHA didn't have money to defend, and his lawyers kept filing so NRHA would have to come up with money to defend. He was intentionally trying to break NRHA financially."

Dick asked Ben to meet him at the airport in Columbus, Ohio. Ben picked him up and they drove to the Holiday Inn where Dick had rented a meeting room. Dick sat down and opened his briefcase, which held a large bottle of Crown Royal. He set it on the table between them and, in his words, "When the Crown was gone, Ben called his lawyer and canceled the lawsuit."

In return, Dick had to make a few concessions. One was to put Ben on the NRHA

Lifelong partners and friends, Dick and Brenda Pieper are considered top hands by their peers—trainers, reiners, cutters, event judges, horse breeders, competitors, and horse enthusiasts of every description.
JOHN BRASSEAUX

Board. The other was to do something about the judging system. John Snobelen of Toronto was on the board at that point and he and Dick got together and began to work on that new system, which they patterned after the Olympic system for judging figure skating and gymnastics.

Although they faced as much opposition as they had support, the two persevered on the project. When their system was used experimentally at the NRHA Derby in St. Paul, Minn., most people were pleased with those results and the system was adopted by the NRHA.

Another change during Dick's presidency was moving the NRHA Futurity to Oklahoma City from Columbus, Ohio. The premier event for reiners had been held at the All American Quarter Horse Congress every year except one, but was outgrowing the facility's capacity for stalls and warm-up space. The NRHA administration had been quietly looking for options.

When the National Finals Rodeo left Oklahoma, Dick and NRHA Executive Director Butch Shaver were approached by representatives about the idea of moving the event to Oklahoma City. Talks ensued. Dick remembers, "The Congress gave the NRHA $5,000 a year and Oklahoma City offered a 5-year contract giving us $100,000 per year. We told the Congress administration that because of the long tradition with NRHA and Ohio Quarter Horse Association, in spite of the huge offer, the NRHA was willing to stay if they could just be given any kind of increase and stall concessions. When the Congress was unwilling to do so, the decision was made to move the futurity to Oklahoma City."

It was another controversial decision. Dick explains, "The large concentration of reiners east of the Mississippi felt the move would never work. Ultimately, though, the more central location opened up the way for West Coast reiners to attend and the NRHA Futurity has grown steadily with support from all over the country."

Change came in Dick's personal life, as well. He had gotten to know Canadian reiner Brenda Hoeltzel and the couple planned to marry at some point.

Between 1976 and 1995, Dick rode 23 horses to finish as NRHA Futurity finalists and was a continual top 20 money-earner each year during that time. He and Brenda planned to go to the NRHA Futurity in 1986, the first year it was held in Oklahoma City. Dick's friend and reining legend Bob Loomis had moved to Marietta, Okla., the January before. He called and said, "I know you're going to be riding in snow and confined to the indoor arena at Willowbrook. Come out a couple weeks before the futurity. I'll have stalls and you can ride outside and we'll go to Oklahoma City together."

Dick remembers, "That first morning—it was mid-November and we're driving down from town—windows down—the air was nice. Brenda said she really liked the area. We went to lunch with Bob and she mentioned that. Bob said there was a nice place down the road with a log house on it and the people really wanted to sell."

Dick and Brenda bought the place, moved to Oklahoma and married in 1987. Their new ranch, halfway between Oklahoma City and Fort Worth and a mile off interstate 35, was a perfect place to market and sell horses. They began to improve and add on, with an eye to establishing a breeding facility.

They bought a young Colonel Freckles son, Texas Kicker, the next spring at the L.A. Waters Quarter Horses dispersal sale. Dick showed Texas Kicker to the reserve championship of the Reno Spectacular and to become the 1991 AQHA Junior Reining World Champion, and he became the senior stallion on the ranch.

As a reiner, Dick was in that rarified iconic position that few achieve. Acclaimed at the top of the horse industry as a trainer, showman, businessman and judge, he was in demand for clinics and for training both horse and riders.

Although Dick was a reining specialist, he had always had a love for cutting, competing occasionally. When he and Brenda went to 1992 yearling sales in Fort Worth during the National Cutting Horse Association Futurity, they found their new sire prospect. Dick explains, "What we would always do was go to Fort Worth each year and we'd each get a catalog. We'd go off by ourselves and then we'd come back and meet and compare notes. We'd only consider the ones we both liked."

As they came walking together that year, each asked the other, "Did you see that gray yearling colt out of Miss Silver Pistol?" They bought the colt named Playgun and took him home to train.

The change to specializing in cutting came in part because of Playgun's incredible success. Trained and shown by Dick and by cutting horse trainer Jody Galyean, Playgun was the high-money-winning 4-year-old in the National Cutting Horse Association in 1996. He was also the high-money-earning stallion for all ages and in all divisions. During Playgun's event career he won five major events and was reserve champion in three, placing in a total of 21 premier events. His foals have won more than $8 million today. "So many people wanted to breed to him and we felt it was a big part of our business. It was difficult to do both cutting and reining, so the focus of the business shifted into the cutting area."

To the cutting, Dick brought something extra, the thoughtful, foundation of training that had given his reiners incredible show-ring longevity in a discipline where that was a rarity. His technique of training, based on creating a method of communication at increasingly higher levels, has been just as successful in training cutters as it has been in training reiners, and his methods have been copied by many of the top cutters in the industry.

Profile
Cheryl Cody

Cheryl Magoteaux Cody always has had a passion for horses and has had one of her own from the time she was 5. Although her father's Air Force career meant that the family moved regularly, her parents always managed to keep her horses close by except for a stint in Europe.

Cheryl attended the University of Alabama in Birmingham, majoring in English and math, and used her rodeo earnings to help pay her way through college. She created and taught a college horsemanship program, then founded a publication focusing on rodeo in the southeastern United States before taking the job of national media director for the International Professional Rodeo Association.

She began writing for both equine industry and mainstream publications when her daughter, Savannah Magoteaux, was born in 1985. "It was a way to spend more time with Savannah," Cheryl says.

Since then she has written, edited and shot photographs for a range of publications, earning national awards and recognition for both photography and writing. She teamed with barrel-racing legend Charmayne James to write *Charmayne James on Barrel Racing* for *Western Horseman* books and has written for various books in the *Western Horseman* Legends series. Currently Cheryl has two new projects in the works, one a fiction book with a horse-industry background and the other a profile of the Josey Ranch, owned and operated by rodeo legends Martha and R.E. Josey.

Cheryl also is known for her award-winning photography, most notably of the great Hollywood Dun It and other outstanding reining industry stallions. She provided color commentary for *Waltenberry's Reining Video Monthly* and later for *Wide World of Horses*. At the time the program, which Cheryl owned with partner Jack Covington, was the highest-rated equine program on RFD-TV.

Cheryl Cody has devoted a lifetime to the horse industry.
PHILLIP CODY

Cheryl's publication career expanded when she became editor of *Performance Horse* magazine, ultimately accepting the reins and managing the publication, where she accomplished a 300-percent upturn in revenue. After leaving the publication during 2001, she began to develop her own company, Pro Management, Inc., into an innovative mainstay of the Western performance-horse industry. Through the years, she has provided management; advertising; and publishing, media and publicity services for some of the giants in the Western horse industry, including the National Reining Breeders Classic; McQuay Stables; and the National Reining Horse, American Quarter Horse, Southwest Reining Horse, and National Reined Cow Horse Associations. Cheryl now serves as a consultant for other top events.

She and her team have managed and developed some of the largest equine events in the world, including the National Reining Breeders Classic, United States Equestrian Team Reining Championships and the National Reined Cow Horse Association

Snaffle Bit Futurity, World's Greatest Horseman and others.

In addition to her success in the business end of the industry, Cheryl has been active inside the competitive arena, as well. She was an instructor for R.E. and Martha Josey's schools and clinics, and with Martha created the highly popular monthly motivational newsletter, *The Winner's Edge.*

Cheryl is a past Professional Women's Rodeo Association barrel-racing national champion, Women's National Finals Rodeo qualifier, barrel-racing futurity champion and reserve champion, as well as multiple finalist at the American Quarter Horse Association World Championship Show and a reserve champion in Palomino Horse Breeders Association world-show competition.

Cheryl's experience of having a sister and other loved ones impacted by cancer led her to partner with Shorty Koger and Tracie Anderson to found Rein In Cancer, a nonprofit foundation, which in it's first five years raised more than a million dollars. The funds allowed the endowment of the Shirley Bowman Nutrition Center at Oklahoma City's Charles and Peggy Stephenson Cancer Center, as well as direct payments to cancer patients in the equine industry. Cheryl serves as president of Rein In Cancer.

Cheryl and her husband, cattle broker Phillip Cody, live north of Stratford, Okla., on a ranch, which is home to a commercial cattle operation, as well as a "barn full of barrel horse prospects."